city veg

Cinead McTernan: For Hal
Tory McTernan: For George, Ava and Paul

city veg

inspiration from an urban garden

Cinead McTernan

BLOOMSBURY WILDLIFE
LONDON · OXFORD · NEW YORK · NEW DELHI · SYDNEY

BLOOMSBURY WILDLIFE
Bloomsbury Publishing Plc
50 Bedford Square, London, WC1B 3DP, UK
29 Earlsfort Terrace, Dublin 2, Ireland

BLOOMSBURY, BLOOMSBURY WILDLIFE and the Diana logo
are trademarks of Bloomsbury Publishing Plc

First published in the United Kingdom 2022

A catalogue record for this book is available from the British Library.

Library of Congress Cataloguing-in-Publication data has been applied for.

ISBNs: HB: 978-1-4729-8784-6; ePub: 978-1-4729-8783-9; ePDF: 978-1-4729-8785-3

2 4 6 8 10 9 7 5 3 1

Designed by Austin Taylor
Printed and bound in China by RR Donnelley

To find out more about our authors and books visit
www.bloomsbury.com and sign up for our newsletters.

Contents

A note about my garden

My city plot measures a compact 4.5m by 3.5m, or approximately two classic 1970s VW camper vans, parked side by side. Despite its size, I fancifully think of it as a miniature walled garden (although with more than 25 windows overlooking it, it's not quite the bucolic setting you might expect for a traditional vegetable plot of this kind). Aesthetics aside, it's surrounded on three sides with brick walls, which are about 1m high – although two of them are topped with wooden fencing, which makes them another half-a-metre taller – and bifold doors, which lead out onto the garden from the kitchen, meaning the fourth side is predominantly glass.

As the garden is one in a terraced row, it's fairly sheltered and enjoys a microclimate all of its own, which is really helpful when it comes to growing fruit and vegetables.

South-east facing, it gets a good amount of sunlight. The area closest to the house (the small patio and one of the square-shaped raised beds) gets the morning sun and is in full shade by midday, while the remaining two-thirds of the plot enjoys around eight hours of sunshine in summer. A base of clay soil prompted me to create three raised beds, two of which are 1m square and the third measures 1m by 3m. Two amelanchiers, three espalier apple trees and a huge ball-shaped bay are planted in the ground. I have also squeezed in a container-grown strawberry tree as well as a standard myrtle. Together they provide something in the way of an edible harvest with either berries, leaves or fruits appearing throughout the year. I'm also lucky to have a small greenhouse (it's actually a hybrid: half-greenhouse, half-shed), as well as a medley of containers filled with various bulbs, annual and perennial crops. I should also include my neighbour's apple tree, which hangs over our hedge – we are allowed to pick any apples on our side.

Food for thought

Growing edibles in an urban plot will influence the type of crop you can grow, as well as how you'll grow them.

In 1900, less than 14 per cent of all people lived in cities; today more than half of the world's population live in an urban setting. This will only increase in the coming decades. By 2100, the population of the UK is predicted to grow to 82.4 million, and it is estimated that 80 per cent will live in urban areas. In view of this, where space to grow your own is limited, it makes sense to have a good understanding of how to get the best from your back yard or window box. There's no point trying to grow potatoes, which prefer space and are cheap to buy, when you might do better trying a compact variety of a heavy-cropper, like courgettes, which can be used in any number of ways in the kitchen (the age of the spiraliser has certainly made things more interesting) and, when you get sick of the sight of it, swapped for other produce grown by friends.

Victory gardens are useful blueprints to consider. Created during the Second World War when being self-sufficient was more than a whimsical idea to move to the countryside and buy a smallholding, they were built on a needs-must basis – so much so that the government set up an education programme to help households grow their own food, from preparing the soil to harvesting and storing crops. The food shortages resulting from the war had created a pressing need to find a way of feeding the nation – or getting the nation to feed itself. Although we're not at war today, there are many parallels that can be drawn to explain our collective desire to look at gardens, or any outside space, as an opportunity to provide edible crops: the climate emergency, a global pandemic, an economic crisis on the horizon and, thanks to Brexit, possible rising food prices – take your pick!

My 10-year-old son, Hal, and I are vegetarians, and want to grow a variety of crops in our city garden to inspire us to eat more greens (well, if I'm honest, to encourage him to do this), and more generally, to provide us with as much seasonal veg as possible, given the limited space we have. In the following pages, I've recorded our progress – and my thoughts – over the course of a year, from designing the garden in January to harvesting and using our home-grown produce right up until December*.

Whether you decide to get fully involved and construct your own raised beds and watering system, or whether you simply get round to planting those bulbs you forgot about in the cupboard, I hope you find our journey useful and enjoy it as much as we have.

Safety

I'm lucky I don't have any allergies (that I'm aware of anyway), but please do be careful and be sure you're safe to grow, pick and eat (or even touch!) any plant, berry, mushroom or foraged bounty mentioned in this book. For example, the 'Dieta' sweet lupins are not suitable for people with nut allergies.

When you're out and about foraging, it is vital that you correctly identify the spoils before sampling them. There are many toxic plants and fungi in the UK, some of which are potentially deadly.

I garden organically, so I don't have to worry about keeping any bottled nasties out of reach of Hal or the pets – if you choose to use chemicals, however, exercise the necessary safety measures when it comes to using and storing them, and to be honest, while you're at it, have a think about whether or not you really need to use them at all.

* Please note, for the purposes of this book we follow the calendar months of the year, so the detail for some winter suggestions can be found at the end, in the December entries.

Winter

Force rhubarb. (You could also try chicory and/or sea kale.)

Sow broad beans, early peas and Brussels sprouts in the
greenhouse or on a windowsill.

Sow cauliflower, onions, leeks, tomatoes, aubergines, celery and
plant rhubarb in a heated greenhouse or on a warm windowsill.

Transplant October-sown lettuce.

Remove yellowing leaves from your brassicas, as they may harbour pests
and diseases. Earth them up to prevent them from rocking in the wind.

Store garlic, onions and maincrops such as potatoes and carrots.

Protect the exposed tops of celery with straw.

Plant fruit: bare-root trees, bushes and canes.

Prune apple trees.

Move strawberries indoors.

Pot up mint root to force indoors.

Group pots and containers together to help provide
a bit of extra protection against the elements.

Clean the greenhouse and your tools.

Clear away debris, and continue digging and composting
if weather permits.

Forage to make edible gifts such as sloe gin.

Incorporate well-rotted manure to feed the soil before it freezes.

January 1st

A new year, a new start

While I'm all for encouraging new gardeners to grab a spade and get planting, I'm not sure about writing a grow-your-own book which approaches the subject as a how-to guide, implying that if you do everything suggested in the book, you will achieve the 'perfect' garden, filled with healthy, vigorous plants yielding year-round bumper harvests.

Perhaps a better start would be: *Please have realistic expectations about growing your own if your plot, like mine, is relatively small.*

The truth is (and let's face it, we need to champion honesty in a post-Trump era), this *is* the reality. When it comes to growing fruit and vegetables, there is a direct ratio between space and yield: The more space you have, the more you'll have to eat. It really is that simple. If you have room for only one or two bean plants, you will harvest enough beans for a few meals (assuming you're a couple and not a family of four). Limited space also means you'll be limited with the type of crops you can grow – more so if you're not blessed with six or more hours of sun – and forget design; swanky principles often go out the window if the aim is to squeeze in as much as possible.

At this point, if you haven't muttered 'Bah!' and put the book down in response to this frank appraisal of growing your own, then I'd say the future looks pretty rosy for you and your plot. You're clearly the type of person for whom growing *something* is better than not growing anything at all. If you have a small garden (back or front), a balcony or just a windowsill, you're not going to reap the same bounty that a lucky so-and-so with a bigger veg patch will enjoy, but I would argue that the sense of satisfaction from producing a modestly sized harvest in restricted conditions will be greater.

If you're interested in a plant-based diet (wherever you might be on the spectrum of vegan to flexitarian), eating home-grown fruit, vegetables and herbs is to be celebrated. From the more prosaic objective of saving money (though, to be clear, this isn't a huge factor in small-scale veg growing) to taking an active part in this planet's future, making the decision to grow your own is as much a state of mind as it is nourishment for body and soul. By growing crops, you're working in harmony with nature, providing food and habitats for all manner of wildlife and insects. It's also about time: making time, being patient and taking a moment, whether snatched or savoured, to notice the seasons and see what magic Mother Nature weaves come rain or shine.

As a parent, I want to debunk the notion that growing vegetables will miraculously make your children eat *all* their greens. I have photographs of my son as a toddler, holding the freshly picked carrot he'd been allowed to pull to keep him occupied while I interviewed a couple of inspiring allotmenteers for a magazine feature. He's sown countless seeds, planted plugs and harvested all manner of crops, and yet we still clash about what vegetables he will actually *eat*. But he *knows* his onions ... and his fennel, and various types of tomato. He understands the effort involved in growing a plant from seed, and the time it takes to produce an edible crop. He is aware of how we're not the only ones to find our brassicas a tasty treat, and that a long, hot summer means it's his job to get out the hose first thing in the morning, before the sun hits the garden. These are all things that are vital for the health and well-being of our children and our children's children, not to mention a benefit to the

wider environment. I would venture that a few sides of corn or a handful of beetroot, a scattering of fresh salad leaves throughout the year and a party's-worth of strawberries for a sensational Eton mess, aren't the only rewards to enjoy when you grow your own. The American poet Ralph Waldo Emerson summed it up perfectly when he wrote, 'Life is a journey, not a destination'. So often, arriving ends up being less of a reward than the process of actually *getting there*.

While I've tried to include as much practical information as possible to help you grow a variety of crops, to my mind there's more to consider. It's helpful to know that you sow peas in individual pots, or carrots in rows 5cm apart, however, this information is at your fingertips. There are wonderful guides written by my more-knowledgeable friends and colleagues (see recommended reading on page 283), all of which will get you off to a flying start, not to mention endless websites and YouTube videos, and the seed packets and plant labels themselves that impart the necessary information. But I believe if you really want to get the most out of your growing space, it's worth thinking about the Bigger Picture.

It stands to reason that the broader your understanding of the subject, the more proficient a grower you'll become. After all, we've been doing it since time immemorial, so there's plenty to draw on. Much of growing comes down to personal experience, and what works for one grower might not suit another. The more we understand the subject as a whole, the more we can make informed decisions about when *we* should sow a particular seed or harvest a specific crop, which variety to choose and where to sow or plant it. There's also much to learn if we look back over the centuries, when crops were grown in season and without chemicals, with the aim of modestly sustaining a family or community without wreaking havoc on the local environment.

Perhaps our approach to growing should allow for us to rethink how we do things and evaluate whether received wisdom really is the *best* approach. Maybe this is the moment to dig a little deeper, engage more wholeheartedly and see how the natural world interconnects, and how our actions, however small and seemingly insignificant, can make profound changes?

Veganuary

Eating a plant-based diet is fast becoming the sensible, healthy solution to combat obesity and other issues related to lack of nutrition, as well as for protecting the environment and helping to fight climate change. A 2019 report on climate change and land for the UN's Intergovernmental Panel on Climate Change estimated that a quarter of global emissions come from food production and more than half of these emissions are from animal products. The report concluded that the West's high consumption of meat and dairy produce is fuelling global warming. It's not surprising, then, that more of us want to grow our own, not only to trace our food provenance and learn to eat seasonally, but also to cut back on carbon emissions, air miles and packaging.

It's worth clarifying that a plant-based diet doesn't mean that you are vegetarian or vegan and never eat meat or dairy – all foodies are welcome here. But it does suggest that you will be interested in foods primarily from plants, which include, of course, fruit, vegetables and herbs, as well as unprocessed cheese, nuts, seeds, oils, whole grains, legumes and beans. You'll also be getting more fibre in your diet, as meat doesn't contain fibre, whereas plant-based foods contain them in abundance, providing a great way to feel full after a meal and reducing the need for snacking.

Essentially, in order to maintain balance, a plant-based diet should include a large portion of vegetables (potatoes aren't included in this food group), fruit and whole grains (choosing wholewheat bread, wholegrain pasta and brown rice rather than refined white bread, pasta and rice), combined with reducing (or eliminating) red meats and processed meats and cheese, and replacing them with fish, poultry, beans and nuts.

The garden pantry

A plant-based diet will introduce you to an array of delicious and nutritious ingredients, many of which can be grown at home. In addition to vitamins and minerals, protein (a source of energy) is a key food group that needs to be maintained in a reduced meat or meat-free diet. You might be surprised to discover that the brassica family – leafy greens like kale, spinach, broccoli and cauliflower – are not only rich in vitamins and minerals, but are a source of protein too. Then there are grains like quinoa, amaranth (which produces seed and leafy greens), wheat, millet, rye, spelt, oats, corn, barley and buckwheat, and seeds like sunflower, pumpkin and the more unusual chia and flax, which are a great source of protein and perfectly possible to grow. Nuts are on the protein-rich list, and if you go for something like hazel, you won't need an entire woodland to produce a decent crop – one tree should do it, and is a realistic option for a small-sized garden and even a balcony, if you can accommodate a large container.

Then there are the indoor crops, such as alfalfa, mushrooms and even parsley, which are a good source of protein and will fit on a windowsill.

It's surprising what we can actually grow in our climate – and I suppose it stands to reason that if quinoa is now grown on a commercial scale in this country, producing a container's worth at home isn't unrealistic. I'm noticing that our changing tastes are reflected in the choice of crop offered by the seed companies and specialist plant nurseries, which offer a really interesting choice if you're prepared to dig a little deeper to source seeds and plants. I've tried to cover as many of these as I can in this book, some of which are crops I've grown for years, and others, like grains, I'll be trying for the first time. I'll still have to visit my local health food and vegetable shops for supplies, but that won't detract from the special meals throughout the year, which will be made from our home-grown crops.

Grains

My sister likes to tease me when I make Yvette van Boven's delicious quinoa apple cake (see page 183), or an orange and almond cake with spelt, but she also loves eating the dishes, so I'll forgive her. Using grains as a source of protein is a relatively recent departure from the more obvious pulses, soy and tofu.

A flurry of brilliant cookbooks written around the subject of having a 'healthy gut' inspired me to use more grains, but it wasn't until I caught part of a food series, where the television presenter seemed perfectly happy to recreate a human digestive system using a sausage casing, that I was spurred on to fine-tune my diet. It still haunts me to this day, but the gist of the demonstration was to illustrate how our digested food travels

Vegetarianism and veganism: a potted history

Eating a plant-based diet is not a modern concept. Anthropologist and conservationist Dr Richard Leakey makes the case that our prehistoric ancestors started off eating nuts, seeds and wild cereal staples because they wouldn't have been able to pull flesh apart using only their hands, let alone chew it (we lacked the necessary large canines). Leakey believes that they would have only turned to meat out of necessity when supplies of their usual food ran short. He also suggests that early farmers in the Neolithic period ate a largely plant-based diet, with meat consumed only on special occasions.

By the time of the ancient Indian Vedic period, as early as 1500 BC, a vegetarian diet was actively encouraged. Early vegetarian celebrities include the artist Leonardo da Vinci, while the Vegetarian Society of the United Kingdom was founded in 1847. Almost a hundred years later, in August 1944, when the society was unsuccessfully lobbied to include a section of non-dairy vegetarianism in its newsletter, Donald Watson, secretary of the Leicester branch, coined the term *vegan* (based on the first three and last two letters of 'vegetarian' because to Watson, it marked 'the beginning and end of vegetarian') and produced a publication called the *Vegan News*. During the 1960s, the movement gained momentum when counterculturists used their eating habits, among other things, to promote social and environmental improvements. Over the following years, books like Michael Pollan's *The Omnivore's Dilemma* and *The Vegetarian Epicure* by Anna Thomas promoted the virtues of a plant-based diet, and in 2016, the Plant Based Foods Association was founded in the United States, while Plant-Based Health Professionals UK was formed in 2017.

through our guts to its final destination and, depending on the diet, the digested matter either travelled quickly and with ease, or slowly and with difficulty. I hope you get the picture, I don't want to have to spell it out here. I'm not a nutritionist and I won't digress too much into this area, but my understanding is that by replacing refined carbohydrates (white bread, white pasta, starchy potatoes) with grains, I have made some improvement to my gut health. For me the (unscientific) proof was in the fact that I no longer felt so bloated and lethargic, and instead found I had more energy and wanted to exercise more regularly.

I was astonished to discover that, in theory, grains can be home-grown – I had assumed that without the equivalent of an acre field 'out the back', it wouldn't be worth my while. It turns out that roughly 90 square metres – just under half a tennis court – will produce approximately 25kg (about a bushel) of wheat, which, once milled, makes 90 loaves. For many, that's still a farm-sized crop, but another way of looking at this calculation is that a large trough-style container, or a row in a vegetable plot, will produce enough of a harvest to reward your efforts.

I have just ordered several packets of different varieties to try – one or two in the raised beds, and the others in containers. I'm so excited at the prospect of growing my own grains ... though I can only imagine what my sister will say.

Buckwheat

Firstly, I need to address the issue that buckwheat is technically *not* a grain – it's something called a pseudo-cereal – but it's widely regarded as a grain because it shares the same culinary and nutritional values. From a horticultural point of view, it's also a green manure. In other words, it's a crop that can be grown to benefit the soil by digging it back into the earth before it flowers. It's versatile too, and can be sown in March and dug in in June to help feed the soil and break up heavy clay, or sown in summer to give the soil a rest and dug in in November. If you're looking to harvest the seed (which is the grain we eat), you'll either have to leave some or the entire crop to flower and go to seed. You could also grow it in a large container, but keep in mind it produces long roots, so make sure it's a deep container. It grows well in poor soil and is fast growing, maturing in just 75 days. They're fun to harvest – simply cut the stems and lay them on a clean sheet and whack them with a broom or something similar to help dislodge the seeds.

Millet

I ordered black millet, which is a food staple in Africa, Central America, and South Asia. It's a lovely plant, a little like corn, and will provide height and interest to borders or container displays. Millet is a good choice if you have space to grow in the ground but your soil is poor. It's also a useful crop because it can be sown in spring or summer, whenever there's a gap, and matures quickly – in as little as 30 days. To harvest, pick and then separate the grains from the plant by rubbing between your hands. I will cook this grain, treating it like brown rice, but I've also read you can pop the seeds like popcorn, and the flour is a gluten-free alternative for making bread, but you'll need a heavy-duty coffee grinder.

Quinoa

This is another pseudo-grain, which I love and often use at home as an alternative to rice, mixed with other grains in a salad, and even disguised in the aforementioned apple cake, which Hal will happily eat. I'm going to try a 'Rainbow' variety, which promises a colourful display when the seed ripens in September/October. It thrives in wet, cold weather and reaches about 2m, so it's really best sown directly in the ground after the last frosts and when the soil has warmed up a little. I am going to allocate a small square patch for this in the bed in front of the greenhouse. I'm hoping to squeeze it in next to the fennel, which will mean digging up and dividing the catmint to make space.

I've also made a note to try rye, spelt and 'freedom' oats at some point as these grains like a cold, wet climate.

January 4th

The best-laid plans...

Our combi boiler, which broke down on Friday leaving us without hot water or heating, has thankfully just been repaired. Obviously I'm relieved that I can finally cast off three of the four jumpers I've been wearing over the weekend, along with the woolly hat and a lovely new scarf my friend made me out of recycled scraps of cashmere, but I've been cheated out of the perfect opportunity to sit down in front of the fire (our only heat source), surrounded by books, magazines and my tablet, to indulge in an hour or so of vegetable garden planning. I had tried to do it over the weekend, but never quite found the time – now the house is warm once again, I don't feel I can justify creating such a cosy scene in the middle of the day. I've lost track of the times I've written about January being the perfect month to spend time designing your garden in exactly this way, but I've never managed it myself. My attempts at creating a design for our plot are always fairly last-minute, which is a shame, because careful planning, especially in a small space, really does pay dividends.

The main thing to think about when planning your plot is what it is you actually have to work with. It helps if you've been able to study it over the year, so that you know where the first of the sun's rays fall, where the frost lingers and which plants might be affected by strong winds. It's really interesting to see how your plot changes with each season, and keeping note of all its quirks and characteristics will help you sow and plant with the confidence that you've given your crop the very best chance to thrive.

If you are discovering your plot for the first time, general rules of thumb will apply – and in fact are more applicable to a small space, as

The best-laid plans...

27

there is less possibility of fluctuating temperatures and idiosyncratic light levels – so finding out which direction your garden or balcony faces is a good start.

Establishing what type of soil you have will dictate your plans, too – not only which plants you can grow, but also what they can be grown in. If, for example, the soil is heavy clay, you might want to grow veg in raised beds filled with more accommodating topsoil. While soil structure can be improved and even changed over time, coping with heavy clay or poor, sandy soil is an uphill battle and an alternative approach to growing might be a sensible, and ultimately time-saving option. The same can be said for water levels in your plot – a soggy patch is hard to regulate (unless it's caused by a leak) so unless you fancy growing watercress or rice, it might be worth building raised beds here too (see page 29).

Once you've established these fundamentals, it's then a case of deciding what you'd like to grow. Are you experimental and interested in trying more unusual crops that are hard to buy in supermarkets and shops? Or perhaps you hanker after the taste of home-grown tomatoes – a flavour that is hard to find from intensely farmed crops, which are either

firm and tasteless or soft and overly sweet. Does a weekly harvest appeal to you or are you looking to pep up home-cooked dishes with fresh herbs and spices? I think it's worth saying again here that the idea of being sustainable in terms of fruit and vegetables is a stretch, and it all depends on the size of your family as well as the quantity of fresh produce you consume. My aim for this book was to grow a variety of seasonal veg that would allow us to harvest something once a week throughout the year, this taking centre stage each week, and allowing us to enjoy a sense of seasonality, as well as the fun of finding something to eat in our own back yard. Deciding why you're growing will help you formulate a design.

While these practical considerations form the foundations of your design, there is plenty of opportunity for you to be creative – though again, using design to solve practical issues involving space is a good starting point (think pleached or lollipop-shaped trees to allow for growing space beneath them) rather than designing around something that is really just a gimmick (think planting in wellies and vintage cans of Heinz tomato soup).

Your list contains the building blocks of your design because you'll know the best spot for each

crop you're hoping to grow (they'll either be sun-loving or shade-loving plants). The next step is to get some inspiration, by looking in books, online and even over your neighbour's fence. Be realistic about your budget – a container garden is a good idea but might require a bit of imagination to fill it with recycled receptacles if numerous (and expensive) shop-bought containers are out of the question. Raised beds are a good option if budgets are tight, either making them from recycled, free materials or buying inexpensive wood. They don't have to be raised to great heights – mine are 30cm or so high, which was just enough to allow me to add organic matter and some good topsoil and to keep them topped up with rich, nutritious soil. You can put them on hard ground (paving or concrete), but make sure they're deep enough to provide ample soil for roots to grow. Alternatively, you can put them directly on grass and, of course, bare earth. If your raised beds are deeper than 50cm, add a layer of hardcore to help with drainage – this also helps reduce the amount of soil you need to use. You will also need to dig foundations if you're building brick or stone walls higher than 20cm. Think about how you access your growing areas – do you need to make a path? Is there room to add a table and chair and if so, are you a sun worshipper or do you prefer the shade?

How do you describe yours?

North-facing is another way of saying a shady garden – dark and damp in a lot of cases – but this isn't all bad news for veg growers as there is a decent bunch of herbs, fruit and veg that will put up with murky conditions.

South-facing and you've hit the jackpot because your plot will be bathed in light from sunrise to sundown, which means you can grow anything, even if it needs a bit of shade, because this can be created by planting a tree or resorting to an artificial shade sail or something similar.

East-facing means that the sun will shine in your plot during the morning – great if you're an early bird who will enjoy a cuppa looking out at your sun-kissed crops first thing. In the main, during the height of summer, your crops should get enough sunlight to produce a respectable harvest.

West-facing gets afternoon and evening light, so a similar story to that of an east-facing plot, other than the fact that your brew will be craft beer rather than tea.

Mulching and hotbeds

Today we find ourselves in national lockdown for the third time. It's a strange feeling. We've been here before, obviously, but there are differences that make it unfamiliar. There is a vaccine, but there is also an air of uncertainty, with talk of new strains of the Covid-19 virus, which has already had such a devastating impact on the world since we all first heard of it in 2020. As with so many times in my life when things appear overwhelming or unsettling, I find comfort in my

garden. During the first lockdown, both Hal and I enjoyed our back yard because the weather was glorious and I had bought an outdoor sofa the day before the prime minister announced the restrictions. Breakfast, lunch and ice creams were eaten al fresco and in comfort. We read, played cards and, on a few occasions, stargazed on the more balmy evenings, lying on the sofa under blankets. The garden became another room for us, and we benefited from the connection with nature that comes with being outside. This time around, it's not the weather for lazing about outdoors, nor ideal conditions to garden: the ground is too hard and the air temperature too cold for planting, much less seed sowing. However, I'm keen that we get an outdoor fix, while keeping within the guidelines of lockdown. Thankfully we have an estuary a short drive away, so we're heading there to get some exercise and collect a small bucket of seaweed while we're at it. I'm also hoping the stables that sell well-rotted horse manure will be open.

The combination of manure and seaweed is a fantastic – and free – mulch that revitalises and nourishes the soil in my veg borders. I could wait another month or so to mulch the garden, but it feels good to have a sense of purpose to our walk today, and I'll have it to hand to dig into the soil as soon as it warms up a bit.

Mulch

Whether you have borders, containers or window boxes, taking care of the soil is the best way to make sure plants are healthy, strong and able to produce a plentiful bounty of tasty crops. Adding a layer of mulch protects the top few centimetres of soil, which is packed to the gunnels with microorganisms, organic matter and soil nutrients. Biodegradable mulches, or a layer of organic matter, are incorporated into the soil by worms, where they slowly break down over time, releasing their nutrients into the soil, which nourishes plants and improves the soil's structure. Mulch also reduces moisture loss from the soil (by evaporation) and, as it blocks sunlight from the soil's surface, suppresses weeds too.

Garden compost

Whether you make your own (see page 68) or buy it from your local council or garden centre, this crumbly soil packed with nutrients is an excellent mulch. Aim to add a 5cm layer over the soil, being careful to leave a small gap around the base of any soft stems in the border or container to help prevent them from rotting.

Leaf mould

This is an excellent urban resource if you have a local park or tree-lined streets where leaves fall freely (literally) during the autumn, though consider the road pollution and gather leaves from less-busy streets. I don't see why you can't ask your local council sweeper to see if they'd give you the leaves, though it's probably easier to nip out before they hit the streets. These decaying leaves make a fantastic crumbly soil conditioner that is low in nutrients and can be used as a mulch as well as a seed-sowing or potting compost, as it matches the needs of delicate, developing seedlings. Easy to make, it's just a question of gathering leaves in autumn and storing them in a hessian sack or recycled plastic bags with a few air holes punched in them with a garden fork. I manage to make a couple of bin liners' worth each autumn from the two rowan trees we have in my garden, next door's Virginia creeper that trails over the back wall, and other waifs and strays that blow into the plot. I stash them behind the greenhouse in a rota, the oldest at the front, until I want to retrieve the one-year-old stuff, which is perfect to use as a potting mix.

Well-rotted manure

This is 'the good stuff', as my grandad used to tell me – so much so, he'd run out onto the street as a youngster to gather the droppings left in the middle of the road by the horses, so that his dad could spread it on their roses. These days you can buy well-rotted manure (two years or more old) in garden centres and online or go direct to source if you have a local stables. The reason it's so good for roses – and vegetables – is because it's high in nutrients and helps lock moisture into the soil, but it's no good if used fresh, as it can actually scorch plants with its high levels of nutrients.

Seaweed

Containing essential nutrients for plants – nitrogen, phosphate, potassium and magnesium – seaweed has been used to improve coastal soil for centuries. In the main it is a sustainable, renewable resource, but you do have to check with the landowner or local council that you are allowed to collect it from a beach (some beaches are private or areas of special scientific interest). As with all foraging, be thoughtful and only take what you need (think home use not commercial amounts). I also use an organic liquid form of seaweed as a feed, which, from a nutritional perspective, is better than the fresh stuff – though you can't beat a bit of foraging on a wet, wild day at the beach. If the ground isn't too hard, dig in fresh seaweed during winter months, before it dries.

Composted wood chips

This might not look like it would be any good for improving soil, but its bulk is ideal for improving drainage in compacted soil, as well as helping it retain moisture levels. Check you're buying composted wood chip (not the larger, decorative version) and source from reputable garden centres and nurseries that can guarantee the woodchips are sustainable and don't have chemicals added to them.

There are also non-biodegradable – or decorative – mulches, like slate chippings or gravel. These will do everything a biodegradable mulch does, apart from feed the soil. That said, covering winter borders with a dark layer, like an old rug or tarpaulin, will help warm the soil and allow you to start sowing and planting earlier.

Hotbeds

Another use for manure, and inspired by a visit to the magical Lost Gardens of Heligan in Cornwall, is creating your own hotbed, an ideal solution for small-space growing. I saw their Victorian-style pineapple pits in their Melon Yard and the memory of them stuck with me – I loved the structure of the pits, or cold frames, and the idea of growing something so exotic by simply using manure to create an intense heat source stuck with me. Further research revealed that they were originally used to extend the growing season, and to enable salads to be sown and grown in winter.

The idea is straightforward: heat is provided at the base of the bed by manure rather than an electric heat source, and crops are grown in a 20–30cm layer of soil at the top. As a combination of straw and manure breaks down, heat is created and, with a manure to soil ratio of 3:1, you can achieve the optimum growing temperature of 24°C. If the soil becomes hotter than this, you risk scorching plants, but a little water or organic matter can be added to reduce the heat levels. It takes about a week to warm up, and while I created mine in a square container inside the greenhouse, you can also create one outdoors, as long as you insulate the sides of the heap (using pallets) and cover the top. I think mine was too small – I've since read that they should be about 2m by 2m – but it works moderately well and I managed to get some seedlings off to a good start. In terms of space, it is a commitment, but given that it's a way to start growing in January, when you're able to do little else, it might be worth the effort. The hotbed lasts for a couple of months, and afterwards you can distribute the manure and soil around the garden and rebuild, though unless you want to try growing pineapples, the weather should be warmer, allowing you to sow and grow without a heat source.

Once your hotbed is up and running, you can direct-sow (literally sow into the soil where you want them rather than sowing in seed trays and then transplanting) salads, radish and beetroot to grow and mature in the hotbed itself, as well as starting peas and beans off, ready for transplanting outside in spring, and courgettes in early spring, ready to be transplanted when seedlings are large enough to handle. Rhubarb can also be started off in this way in January, if you plant the crowns in a large pot and sink it in the hotbed. Plant out in its final position in the spring when the weather has warmed the soil.

I don't see why you couldn't use a compost heap as a hotbed, as it generates heat. In 2007, Tatton Park in Cheshire restored their original pineapple house (or pinery), first built in 1774, when they grew pots of pineapples plunged into a bed of tanner's bark (a waste product from the tanning industry). As this isn't available today, they use a special mix of oak-leaf compost instead.

A few stems of **chard 'bright lights'** and **cavolo nero**, to be added to a lemon and ricotta cannelloni.

....

Brussels sprouts (a handful, for me).

....

Several **celery** stems and a handful of **thyme**, to flavour a soup. (Soups tend to be a variation around 2 carrots, 1 leek, 1 onion, 1 sweet potato, 1 potato, 3 stems of celery and thyme. Sometimes I add a few lentils in the hope Hal doesn't realise, since he's not keen on them, but not always, as without them it's his favourite soup.)

Understanding your garden

It's raining so hard that the garden is saturated: the soil, tree branches and the brick walls are all oozing a dank, sodden sheen. What better excuse than to disappear into my study for an hour and continue my research for this book?

One of the many fascinating things about growing plants is the myriad philosophies, techniques and approaches that have been written, videoed or talked about on the subject (the piles of books on my desk are testament to that). Gaining a broad understanding of the basic theories is a great place to start and will provide the foundations to become a good grower. After that, apart from a wheelbarrow's worth of prudent guidelines, when it comes to specific practices, it's hard to argue that there is a *right* way and a *wrong* way – I would argue it's more a question of experimenting and finding out what works in *your* particular space.

As a person who, at the best of times, struggles with precision and accuracy, this is one of the many reasons why I love growing. I revel in the freedom of knowing there might well be an optimum date when you should be sowing your peas, but if you are unable to find a window of opportunity to do this until you've nudged into the following month, more often than not, it's still worth sowing them. The important thing is to get your fingers dirty and take the time to notice the results – there's always next year to tweak, improve or completely change your approach. If you're looking for things to neatly go to plan, gardening may well not be for you because there are so many variables, only some of which you can control. In the end, gardening is essentially fairly democratic as everyone is starting on a level playing field. By all means, read around the subject and find out as much as you can about the principles of horticulture, but nothing, and I mean nothing, beats sowing a seed in a pot and seeing what happens.

I believe it's always a good idea to question conventional wisdom. It's astonishing how many established principles don't withstand scrutiny because at some point they were the only solution at hand, and not even the best one at that. This can be said for our approach to growing vegetables. Tradition appears to tell us that when we grow crops, we should strive for neat, tidy rows of the same variety. In an agricultural context, this makes sense and allows for time-saving machinery to till the soil, sow the seeds, weed and harvest crops. However, in a small-scale operation this orderliness isn't necessary. For some it might satisfy a desired aesthetic, but if you think about it, nature doesn't behave in this way. And if Mother Nature doesn't see the virtue of growing like this, perhaps it's worth considering her alternative?

I wouldn't dream of claiming ownership of this idea – far brighter minds than mine advocate the notion of emulating nature. As awareness of the climate emergency and the resulting sense of urgency heightens and we find ourselves in uncertain times, it's understandable that many of us strive to return to a past that existed in synergy with nature, as opposed to humans pillaging it and using up all its supplies.

Over the last 20 years, there has been a slow, steady progression towards more wildlife-friendly and ecologically sound gardens. Where traditionally, gardens were separated into orderly 'zones' – the patio area, borders, the vegetable beds and an area at the bottom of the garden allowed to go wild – the current thinking is to rewild our gardens and, quite literally, blur the lines between each area. While rewilding herbaceous gardens is gaining in popularity, the same principle can be applied to vegetable patches too. You might not think that vegetables do much in the way of providing habitats for wildlife – cabbage white butterflies and caterpillars aren't going to make you feel it's been worth the effort of growing brassicas when it's only to lose them to these pests. However, if you think of cabbage white caterpillars as a food source for birds, namely sparrows and goldfinches, then the food chain begins to creak into motion – add other elements to attract wildlife and connect your outdoor space, and you've created a hubbub of life as opposed to a few isolated crops.

This type of sustainable gardening, bringing together wildlife, edible landscapes and traditional beds, borders and veg patches, creating a perfect environment for nature to thrive while producing food and satisfying an aesthetic, is the guiding principle behind the practice of permaculture. In a small garden, the scope needs to be scaled down, but the principles remain the same. In other words, gardens based on ecological ideas reflect how nature works – food plants that support insects and other wildlife, plants that break up and nourish the soil and edibles that enrich our diets all combine to create a thriving habitat that benefits everyone.

On a larger scale, the other advantage is that gardens adhering to permaculture methodology will require less upkeep – less watering, weeding, pruning, etc. However, on a small scale this is much harder to achieve – if you're planting in containers, watering is an essential part of your weekly ritual (and your daily ritual during dry, hot summers), there's just simply no getting away from it. But in general, viewing your

entire space as an interconnecting habitat and designing with sustainability in mind sounds like a solid foundation to me. What's not to like about working with what nature has to offer, rather than forcing our will on the natural world? It's a much broader subject than I've managed to convey here, but it's well worth delving into on a dreary winter's day.

Observing and recognising the limitations of your plot is hugely helpful and it is enlightening to see what your growing space is like in all seasons so you can work with it. Believe me, there is a huge temptation to grow what you want rather than what will thrive in your own little patch. By all means, experiment – sometimes you might be successful, and I've refused to accept the inevitable more times than I care to remember. Growing sea buckthorn in pots in my inner-city plot rather than a coastal dune once rewarded me with a modest crop of zingy orange fruits, bursting with vitamins and minerals. But I have also consigned many failed crops to the compost bin after they've perished from too much shade or not enough moisture. In the end it's worth letting sense prevail and playing to your plot's strengths. When I had my first garden, I kept a journal. I hadn't intended on doing so, but after receiving three as flat-warming presents, I felt inspired – if not a little compelled – to give it a go. To begin with I was enthusiastic about recording everything – wish lists of seeds, plants and tools, planting combinations I spotted in urban front gardens on my walk to work, seasonal jobs, visiting wildlife – but it wasn't long before I fell behind with my weekly entries. Finding the time to write my thoughts down proved difficult, but taking the time to notice what was happening in my plot never lost its appeal. These days I tend to reach for my camera (or phone), rather than my pen, as a way of keeping a record of my urban plot. I also capture ideas I like in other gardens and take pictures of plants I want to try growing myself. Quick and detailed, a photograph is hard to beat when it comes to recording both small- and large-scale changes in your garden. Whether it's the changing seasons and the effect they have on the shape of beds and borders, or planting combinations for container displays, or to note how the general appearance transforms throughout the year, a picture is an invaluable starting point if you want to hone your design or make significant changes. The pictures don't need to be beautifully framed or technically perfect to tell the story of what happens in your garden throughout the growing season.

Connect your designs and let areas interplay to help the process – if you would love a tree and want to grow plants that appreciate a little shade, make them bedfellows, so that the tree's canopy will shelter your crop. Think of your garden as the sum being greater than its parts. It's also worth recognising the value of each crop and how elements might help each other. This might seem obvious in the example of a tree providing shelter, but planting the tree somewhere where its leaves can fall and nourish the soil might be something you overlook – or perhaps if it's planted in a pot, make a note to gather the leaves in the autumn to make leaf compost, so that nothing is wasted.

The grandfather of permaculture

The word permaculture derives from a contraction of permanent and agriculture, and was brilliantly coined by Australian author (among other things) Bill Mollison. He wrote *Permaculture: A Designer's Manual* (first published in 1988) to share his theory that if humans have lived in harmony with their local environment for millennia, today we must find a way to coexist sustainably.

One of Mollison's students, David Holmgren, worked with him to bring this new concept to a broader audience via his talks, courses and books. Twenty years ago the term permaculture was all but unknown, but today there are courses and books helping spread the idea to more growers and environmentalists.

Another key book and a great read on this subject is Andrea Wulf's *The Invention of Nature*, which tells the fascinating story of scientist and pioneer Alexander von Humboldt, who, when travelling in the early nineteenth century, identified and publicised the folly and wanton destruction of vital natural habitats at the hands of mankind.

Contain your ideas

Throughout my adult life, container gardening has provided a lifeline: when I lived in a rented top-floor flat with a small square roof terrace, or on the ground floor with a good-sized plot that sadly had wall-to-wall paving slabs, locked in place with concrete (I know this because I tried lifting a few in the vain hope of breaking up the endless grey with random herb-filled squares), or in my own home with a minuscule front garden and modest back garden. Whether containers have been the only way I have managed to grow anything, or have enhanced my ground space, adding structure and interest, I wouldn't be without them. I've even grown vegetables in pots for a book themed around popular recipes, *One-Pot Gourmet Gardener*.

I would encourage everyone to add containers, whatever their shape (though not necessarily whatever their size – I'll explain later), to their garden, windowsill or balcony. The trick to successful container growing is being real-istic about which plants you can grow in them and how they need to be looked after – namely feeding and watering during the growing months. Container-grown plants aren't able to put down their roots to reach a natural water source and the level of nutrients and

minerals, which are in abundance as a result of the natural life cycles of the soil, are eventually depleted in a container unless we replenish them. Having learned the hard way, I would urge you to incorporate the two vital tasks of feeding and watering your container-grown crops into your weekly schedule, and if you're away, make alternative arrangements. I can't think of how many crops I've lost because, at a crucial moment, I took my eye off the ball and forgot to water them. It might sound daunting, but it isn't – I'm a disorganised person, so this is something I have to think about, but for those more efficient than me, it's really just a case of putting aside a small amount of time each week.

Size also matters, and in my opinion bigger is nearly always better when it comes to container-grown fruit and vegetables – not only because bigger containers hold more soil, which helps maintain moisture levels for longer and prevents temperatures from fluctuating too much during the summer months, but they also provide more space to accommodate roots and ensure there is leeway to add organic matter if required during the growing season. Cute, quirky pots are fun for kids and a great way to recycle, but I'm not a fan because in practice, there is often not enough soil for the plants to flourish and there's also the issue that they dry out very quickly in warmer weather. If you're not carrying out a daily inspection and they're deprived of water for too long, the plants will become stressed and unhealthy, and they will ultimately perish. There are of course drought-tolerant, shallow-rooted plants like thyme and marjoram that will cope better with this treatment (though I'm not encouraging erratic watering). But essentially, it makes sense to choose carefully in the first place – many crops and plants won't be able to cope in containers that are left to dry out regularly, and if you don't have time to spend watering every day, small pots are best avoided. That said, hanging baskets and window boxes come into their own in so many urban locations, and as long as you're realistic about what will grow well in them and you're diligent about watering them, you will be rewarded with eye-catching displays that will produce bountiful harvests.

I've also tripped up with drainage over the years – it might sound obvious, but unless you're recreating a mini bog garden, you need to ensure

water can drain away from the pot, otherwise roots will sit in waterlogged soil, which weakens and eventually kills the plant. A drill is the best tool to make drainage holes, but I've had moderate success with hammering in nails – though be aware, plastic and resin can shatter, so be careful. The key thing is to make provision for water to seep away – I will leave the detail to you. Don't be tempted to use pebbles or stones in the bottom of the pot as a substitute for holes (again, I have done this). This works fine if you're watering the pots and can control the water level, but when it rains you'll end up with a pot full of water, just as if you had no drainage.

My favourite containers are made from terracotta and concrete, though these materials are porous so do require additional watering. On the downside, they are heavy to move around (especially when planted), retain the heat (ideal for sun-loving but not tender specimens), and are vulnerable to frost, which may cause them to crack (pot-feet work here, keeping them off the ground and away from puddles of water). A fake-effect alternative is a good option and addresses some of the issues, as they are lighter, non-porous and durable. Metal also heats up in the sun, so bear that in mind when choosing the plant and maintaining a watering schedule, while wood is an eco-friendly option (assuming it

has been sourced sustainably and stained or preserved using an eco-friendly product), which offers insulation against soaring temperatures. Plastic isn't ideal – environmentally speaking as well as not allowing the plants to breathe, meaning they generate too much moisture. Black pots can even overheat in high summer and dry out the soil more quickly.

Whichever you choose, containers are a great addition to your garden or balcony. They add height and interest to your outdoor space, are versatile in terms of their position (and can come with you if you move house), and allow you to grow a plant in its favourite type of soil if it requires a particular type.

Watch out for vine weevils

These annoying pests can be the curse of the container-grown crop. Look out for notches in the leaves, which is the tell-tale sign that the dark brown adult beetles are hard at work in the growing season. In autumn and winter, plants might wilt as the white grubs lay waste to the roots. Strawberries are particularly susceptible. Use a nematode, a parasite that feeds on the vine weevils, to beat them at their own game. Treatments that include *Steinernema kraussei* or *Heterorhabditis megidis* are particularly effective, but follow the instructions carefully because they need particular conditions to work well. An evening, torch-lit hunt for adult beetles is often worth the effort as you're likely to catch the culprits in action, and, if you're lucky, before the female has had a chance to lay eggs.

Brussels sprouts (another handful, for me).

....

Several **celery** stems and a handful of **thyme**, to flavour this week's veg soup.

....

A **red cabbage** used in a slow-cooked curry. Simple and delicious... Fry off onion and garlic with spices (any combo of cumin, coriander, garam masala, turmeric), add a tin of tomatoes, a tin of butter beans and the whole cabbage, shredded. Slow roast for a few hours until the cabbage is soft and almost disintegrates. Serve with rice.

Mushrooms

I have a faint memory of growing mushrooms as a child. While I can't remember how we actually did it – a cruel blow for parents who spend agonising amounts of time preparing fun activities for their kids, only to have them consigned to the memory bin in the years that follow – I vaguely recall seeing dazzlingly white little button mushrooms dotted across a tray of soil that had been left to lurk in the depths of our cupboard under the stairs (before this type of cupboard would be forever associated with Harry Potter).

While harvesting fruit and veg from your own back yard is something to be savoured, to my mind, having a supply of home-grown fungi feels a bit like alchemy, and as they will grow indoors, they're a brilliant crop for a space-starved city gardener and so, this winter, I'm trialling two kits.

Needless to say, I didn't get the chance to create a potential memory for Hal to eventually forget – he doesn't like mushrooms and so was less than enthusiastic about the prospect of growing them himself. Undeterred, I gathered the necessary paraphernalia (well, opened the boxes sent to me by the mushroom kit suppliers). It's straightforward, if a little time consuming. (When it comes to growing mushrooms, preparation, it turns out, is key.)

Oyster mushrooms

This kit is essentially a bag of straw with an accompanying bag of spores and a perforated fruiting bag. The first thing to do is soak the straw in about 3 litres of boiling water – I stand the bag in a trug in case it leaks. This needs to be left in its bag for a couple of hours (the smell of steaming straw takes me right back to mucking out stables as a horse-mad 10-year-old ... ha! That memory went the distance). After draining the water thoroughly, I sprinkle the spawn onto the straw and seal the neck of the bag, shaking well to distribute it. The mushroom nursery then moves to a warm (18–25°C), dark spot for four weeks, which in my case is a corner of the kitchen near a radiator. Once the white root-like strands of the mushroom mycelium are visible, the bag needs to be cooled for two days in the fridge. After this I remove the straw from the bag and place it on a shallow tray in a lit area. Temperature wise, anywhere between 10°C and 21°C is fine, so I put them on the counter top in the kitchen. This is where the perforated fruiting bag comes into use as a cover, and I spray water underneath it a couple of times a day to create humid conditions. The mushrooms, which are the fruit of the mushroom fungus, can be picked anywhere between 4 and 10 days later. Mine appeared around the edge of the straw first, so I carefully removed them with a knife so I didn't disturb the straw. The great thing about mushroom growing this way is that the straw can be used again, because the mycelium created had the potential to grow far more mushrooms than space allowed the first time. After this first harvest, I soak the straw in cold water for two hours, drain and place back on the tray, covered by the fruiting bag, and repeat until the straw is exhausted.

Button mushrooms

This is another simple kit comprising a bag of colonised compost in a tray, a cover and a bag of cover soil. The first step is to activate the spores by placing the compost tray and cover somewhere warm (20–25°C) for four days, after which the compost should have turned white with the mushroom mycelium. It's now ready for the compost to be covered with soil, but I need to punch holes in the bag (the instructions rather specifically stipulate 10 on each side!) and leave it to soak in half a litre of water for 30 minutes. The bag can then be opened and the moist soil used to cover the compost in the tray. The covered tray is stored in a warm, dark spot (20–25°C) and left for five to eight days so that the mycelium covers the soil. Once this has happened, it can be moved to a cooler position

(15–18°C). I will allow the mushrooms to reach the size of a 50 pence piece before harvesting (pulling and twisting is the best technique here). Once the first batch of mushrooms has been harvested, I can water the soil again and get up to two more crops.

Outdoor mushrooms

Naturally found in damp, dank, wooded locations, mushrooms can also be grown outside using kits. Try wooden dowels impregnated with mushroom spawn and 'plant' in a hardwood log, such as oak, beech, birch, hazel or willow, about 10–15cm in diameter. Drill holes in rows down the length of the log, 7.5cm apart and at 15cm intervals. Tap in the dowels, keeping them flush to the surface, and cover with wax. Hide in a shady area – under a tree is ideal to protect from wind, rain and sun. A bit of patience is needed as spores can take between six and eight months to colonise a log and appear out of the ground. Just like indoor varieties, grasp by the stem and twist when it's time to pick and enjoy a fresh supply for up to a month. Leave to regenerate for a few months and the log can remain productive for up to six years. Oyster, shiitake and Lion's Mane mushrooms all grow well using this method. You can pick up DIY growing kits from specialists; some suggestions are listed in the resources section at the back of the book.

A few stems of **chard 'bright lights'** to sauté and add to pasta.

....

A few more **Brussels sprouts**, which I will shred and sauté with butter and garlic to add into a quiche.

....

Several **celery** stems as well as a handful of **thyme** and a couple of **bay** leaves, to flavour a veggie shepherd's pie.

Lifting one's spirits

I can't remember the last morning when the garden looked so bright. Over the last weeks my eyes have grown accustomed to the saturated, dreary-brown coloured paving stones, a darker shade in the wet, which set off the whole garden, making it appear damp and dour. Today, however, everywhere is dry and the sky, a weak, watery blue, bathes the garden in a clear, vivid light. It's a magical effect in which everything is thrown into sharp focus.

I feel invigorated. It's so true that a glimpse of spring brings with it a sense of hope and new beginnings. I throw open the windows and plan to spend at least an hour in the greenhouse, sorting out the mess that has accumulated over the winter months, when cold, wet weather made it impossible to linger long enough to stow away tools, seed packets and other bits and bobs in their proper places. As a result, the potting bench is cluttered. Yesterday I noticed a spider had woven her web in the crevice created between an old seed tray and a hastily dumped pile of seed packets.

When the sun shines there's a warmth in the air too, despite an accompanying sharp breeze when it disappears again behind the fluffy, putty-coloured clouds. It's another glorious sign of the changing season.

Nothing to harvest this week, but I'm hoping for
a few **chard** or **kale** leaves next week!

Early sowing

I woke at 6.30 this morning. It's unusual for me to be up before Hal, so I grabbed the chance to make coffee and sneak into the greenhouse before the general chaos of the day took hold (though it was impossible to avoid the weaving cats, winding their tails around my ankles, gently demanding to be fed before I escaped the kitchen and headed out into the garden). The outdoor string of lights provided just enough illumination inside the greenhouse for me to gather a couple of seed trays, a soil scoop and seed packets.

I'm only indoor-sowing early pea and broad bean varieties, but I could also be starting off Brussels sprouts, carrots, radish and even

turnips this month, as well as herbs like thyme, mint and rosemary. (There's no need, because I buy Brussels sprout and carrot plugs to plant out in late April or May and direct-sow radish when the soil has warmed up, usually around April. As for turnips, I've never grown them, and although I've appreciated them once or twice in a stew, I haven't wanted to evict another crop to squeeze them into my plot ... but don't let that stop you, if turnips are your thing.)

'Douce Provence' and 'Waverex' peas are two varieties that you can start off now and enjoy earlier harvests than you would from direct-

sowing in March. Depending on space, the ideal scenario would be to make this early sowing in trays and then sow outside at regular intervals between March and July, so that you spread out when the plump little pods are ready to be picked. I make an early and main sowing, so I can plant another crop in its place in early summer, having enjoyed a few months of picking fresh peas. Alternatively, if you have space, sow 'Douce Provence' (along with a few other hardy varieties) in October, to overwinter in a greenhouse or on a windowsill, ready to get off to a flying start as soon as temperatures warm up in spring.

'Capucijner' is a lovely heritage pea variety, bred by Capuchin monks in the Netherlands in the 1500s, which is really eye-catching as the pods are a blueish purple, but they're best sown in individual pots in March.

Broad beans can be treated in the same way, and there are also varieties that can be sown directly into the ground in November, allowing seedlings to acclimatise ready for warm weather in spring. Our cats trample all over the raised beds, especially during the winter when

there's more bare soil, so I sow in February in pots, ready to plant out in spring. 'De Monica' is one of the earliest broad bean varieties to produce a crop from a spring sowing.

Peas and broad beans don't like their roots to be disturbed, so start them off in modular trays. This way, the roots of the individual seedlings are surrounded by soil and relatively protected.

I planted a cardoon (artichoke thistle) last year to give the corner of the border some year-round structure and soften the edge of the greenhouse. I think there's enough growth this year (I bought a 5-litre pot) to blanch the leaves so I can eat them. I had some large coils of scrunched up paper from bathroom tiles I bought, which was perfect to unscrunch and use

to cover the base of the leaves. In about six weeks or so, I can harvest them as the lack of light will have improved their texture and flavour. If you want to sow seeds, sow in trays in spring and then transplant when the seedlings are large enough to handle.

When it comes to planting the seedlings out, choose a sunny spot in the border or a large container. Fork in some well-rotted organic matter and push half a dozen canes into the soil in a circle, tying them together at the top to create a teepee. Plant a couple of seedlings at the base of each cane. Gently tie in the seedlings as they grow, and pinch out the tips when they reach the top of the canes. Water well and watch out for hungry birds, which might peck out the seedlings, as well as slugs and snails.

SOWING 101

A METHODICAL APPROACH is always best when it comes to sowing indoors. When choosing your seed tray or pot, a useful guide is that trays without divisions are ideal for fine seeds, which are scattered thinly across the surface and can be thinned out later, whereas modular seed trays and 9cm pots are suited to larger seeds, which are more easily sown in ones or twos and prefer their roots to be left undisturbed. Experiment with recycled plastic food trays, egg boxes, loo rolls, takeaway paper coffee cups or homemade newspaper pots.

When it comes to compost you can either use a good shop-bought seed-sowing compost or you can make your own with an equal mix of soil (crumbly topsoil from the garden is fine), homemade compost and leaf mould.

Once you've gathered your seed trays, compost, seeds and tray of water, you're ready...

1. Fill the tray or pot with compost and tap down on a flat surface to remove air pockets and allow the soil to settle. Top up if needs be and then sow as directed on the seed packet.

2. Cover with a little more soil and then water – there are different techniques, so try each one and choose the one that you feel works most effectively: either water the soil before sowing; water with a rose end on the watering can after sowing, being extra careful not to disturb the seeds; or stand the tray or pot in another, larger tray filled with water, leave for a couple of minutes until the soil is moist, and remove. Once watered, find the seeds a spot in the greenhouse, on a windowsill, or other similar light-filled position that is well ventilated but not drafty.

3. Keep an eye on the soil so that it doesn't dry out. Don't be tempted to overwater, as excess moisture can harbour fungi, which causes emerging seedlings to fail (also called damping off). A top layer of specialist mulch called vermiculite or perlite can be used to help protect seedlings from the wet soil and prevent this problem.

4 If your seeds are living in a greenhouse or sheltered spot outside, check regularly for signs of hungry pests that might demolish seedlings. Slugs and snails lurk under pots – these can simply be picked off, and I leave them out on the road for the birds. Another annoying pest that lives in the soil is the

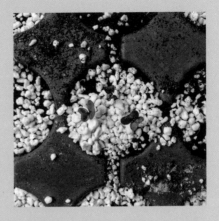

cutworm (or moth caterpillar), which devours the seedlings to the extent that they look like they've been pruned or decapitated. If you push in a cane or stick next to the stem, this makes it harder for the worm to wind itself around the plant and demolish the tasty leaves. Mice can also be an issue – look for droppings, and if necessary, cover seedlings, remembering to ventilate in the day to prevent too much moisture from building up.

5 Once seedlings have reached about 5cm in height, they're ready to be thinned out and/or potted up. The theory behind potting up is to encourage roots to bulk up by filling the vessel they're currently in, so don't be tempted to leap to a large pot immediately. Increase the size of the pots gradually, until the seedlings are strong, sturdy and ready to be planted out in their final position – young roots can't cope with a large volume of compost and tend to rot. I like to put the current pot in the middle of the new pot, filling the gap with soil. Remove the pot containing the seedling (to reveal the right-sized hole in which to plant the seedling) and gently remove the seedling from the pot, including the soil surrounding the roots. Always handle seedlings with care, using the leaves rather than the delicate stem.

If direct-sowing, it's always worth raking and breaking up the soil (you can use a special soil sieve to achieve a very fine crumb). Follow the sowing instructions on the seed packet, water and check regularly for pests.

Early sowing

Something new to try

This year I'm excited to be growing a bean I haven't tried before: 'Dieta' sweet lupin – though I'll have to wait until April before sowing. Here in the UK, lupins are usually grown as an ornamental plant (although in South America they are a traditional food source, which tastes rather bitter), but this variety produces large pods of sweet-tasting nutritious seeds that resemble flattened beans and can be eaten fresh or dried. (Do not eat these seeds if you're allergic to peanuts.)

Special equipment

A heated propagator is necessary in February if you want to start off seeds like tomato, cauliflower, celery, French beans and aubergines, which need bottom heat to germinate at this time of year. While there is an initial outlay, propagators extend the growing season and will reward you with earlier crops. However, they're not essential and you can still grow these varieties, starting them later in the year when temperatures have risen. Or make your own hotbed, if you have the space (see page 35).

A few stems of **kale** (that have withstood the frost) and **chard 'bright lights'** for a warm lentil salad.

The art of making compost

Over the last couple of years I have neglected my three espalier apple trees, and I only have myself to blame for the sorry state I find them in this morning. They are growing in front of a wall that is covered in ivy, and once the apple trees' leaves appear, they blend in with the green of the ivy and it's easy to forget they are there until you spy their beautiful pink-tinged blossom in spring or the red fruits in autumn. Given that they are espaliers, the main problem is that rogue new side shoots have grown too long and in the wrong directions, while the 'trained' horizontal branches (or laterals) require a bit of attention to ensure the espalier's shape is retained.

Depending on your point of view, pruning is either an exact science (and therefore has the potential to be a daunting prospect), the success of which depends on picking the right season, the right branch and the right bud, or it's a great excuse to wield a pair of secateurs to relieve any pent-up stress or anxiety. For me, it's the former, and thankfully my aunt (who is a doyenne of pruning) is always at the end of the phone. For my espaliers, I need to follow the rules that apply to 'renovation' pruning because these trees have been neglected for a couple of years and need more than a quick tidy-up (which should be done in August).

My secateurs are clean but old, so before I get started I sharpen them using a special stone designed for the job – you don't want to be tearing at the wood and contaminating the open wound with rust or dirt. I tackle the wayward new growth first, cutting it back to the main trunk so there's just the original framework left. I also remove a few of the older stems

(spurs) that lead off from the horizontal branches, which are rubbing against each other and are too congested. A satisfying 20 minutes later, the tree is looking more loved and hopefully will reward my efforts with a healthy crop this year. The offcuts are destined for the compost bin, after they've been chopped into smaller sections, which will break down more quickly. If you don't have a compost bin or heap, either ask a friend or neighbour who does (they may be grateful for additional material), or put them in whichever bin or bag your council specifies, to be collected and added to the municipal compost.

Garden compost

Making your own compost in an urban set-up can feel like practising the dark arts. The issue is that for the garden matter and kitchen waste to quickly and efficiently become a rich, wonderful soil, you need to generate heat. Lovely big compost heaps are ideal for this, because the sheer quantity creates its own heat source and ensures the process ticks over nicely. The trouble is, in an urban garden it's a push to find room for a compost heap and more often than not we fall back on compost bins. In theory these are good, but in practice I have found that there just isn't enough material to spark the flames, as it were. In terms of volume, the Royal Horticultural Society (RHS) advises that anything less than 1 cubic metre is 'less effective' although don't let this put you off, making your own compost is all the more satisfying when you've defied the odds. Problems arise if you don't have grass cuttings to bulk out the compost (though it's a balancing act because if you add too many grass cuttings you risk the whole thing becoming a slimy mess) or if your compost bin is enclosed at the bottom and won't allow soil organisms to lend a helping hand (add a spadeful or two of soil as the next best thing). It is a matter of trial and error.

Start by finding a shaded spot for your compost heap or bin, ideally with an earth base (for drainage and soil organisms), wooden sides (pallets are often used) and, if possible, a lid (a few squares of old carpet work well here). Fill with a mix of up to 50 per cent soft green material (annual weeds, vegetable kitchen waste and grass cuttings) and 50 per cent woody brown material (prunings, dead leaves, and if you don't have much of this, shredded paper and cardboard). The compost mix needs to be balanced in order for the bacteria and microorganisms to get to work – too much of one type of material will throw things off. It's often recommended that large amounts of kitchen waste or garden cuttings are aerated with shredded paper or other brown woody material, to prevent them from compacting into a soggy heap. Mix or turn the compost about once a month if possible, as this encourages air to circulate, and moisten during the hot summer months if it becomes dry. Your compost will be ready from anywhere between six months and two years. Obviously as you're constantly adding to it, the first compost will be produced at the bottom, where the material is oldest (hence the sliding flap in a lot of compost bins).

If your heap starts to smell, it's likely there's just too much moisture in it. Check it's protected from rain and add more brown material to keep the air flowing. Flies can also be a problem if it's too moist, or if your kitchen waste is exposed and so accessible to the critters – a simple

solution is to cover vegetable peelings with a layer of brown material when you add them.

To pee or not to pee? Organic gardening guru Bob Flowerdew, a regular on BBC Radio 4's *Gardeners' Question Time*, would say an emphatic yes when it comes to peeing on your heap to help accelerate the decomposition process. This is your call – and possibly depends on whether or not you're overlooked by neighbours! A well-balanced heap shouldn't need this help, but if the material doesn't appear to be breaking down and looks dry and fibrous – and you don't want to get the neighbours' tongues wagging – you can buy accelerators to help speed things up.

Don't be disheartened if space is an issue and a compost bin or heap isn't an option – recycling your kitchen waste and garden cuttings in the municipal compost ticks all the boxes for the environment, if not for your own compost supply. And there are always wormeries...

Wormeries

A wormery is a good way to tackle kitchen and garden waste on a small scale. It's amazing how a handful of special Tiger worms (which aren't regular earthworms) will munch through anything from veg peelings to tea bags, coffee grounds to egg shells, in a matter of weeks, making you the most wonderful compost (worm casts) while they're at it. The excess liquid created can be siphoned off too, and used as a plant feed, much like seaweed or comfrey tea.

My father made me a gorgeous wooden wormery the year before last, and I had some success with it. However, my experience ended in catastrophe because I had nowhere to keep it during the height of summer – I'm ashamed and sad to admit I lost the entire wormery when I went away for a week, which turned out to be a scorcher. However, if you can keep your wormery somewhere warm during the winter and cool during the summer months, then I would recommend them as an eco-friendly way to recycle scraps. I've also come across Subpod Compost Systems – their nifty units are buried in the soil and avoid this issue altogether.

Making a wormery

A wormery is essentially a box with layers of different materials inside to keep the occupants happy. Though you can buy them, the wormery itself is easy to make from recycled products from around your home.

1 Start by getting a large plastic or wooden box with a lid. Make plenty of holes in the lid and in the base using a 12mm drill piece – worms need to breathe and so good airflow is important.

2 Scrunch up sheets of newspaper to make a layer to roughly line the bottom of the box, to prevent the worms from escaping through the holes as well as to absorb excess liquid. Scatter a few generous handfuls of sand over the newspaper (the type that can be used for a child's sandpit is fine) – it doesn't need to completely cover the newspaper, just enough to give a gritty texture to the mix. Next provide the worms with a 'bed' of soil – compost or leaf mould is fine. It's a good idea to make this about 2cm or so thick.

3 You're now ready to add the worms. They are widely available from pet stores, garden centres or online (see the resources list at the end of the book). A kilo of worms is fine to begin with, and once they've settled in, they'll breed and produce enough worms to suit the size of their home. Worms are sensitive to light, so cover them with a little more compost. Provide water using a watering can with a fine rose – you don't want to swamp them, just enough to moisten the soil and newspaper.

4 It's now time to add your kitchen scraps, a layer 5cm thick at the most – worms prefer variety and small pieces of anything vegetable-based is ideal, plus tea bags and coffee grounds. Avoid large quantities of citrus peeling, fatty waste, fish or meat. You can also add garden waste too: prunings and grass cuttings, weeds and deadheaded flowers work well. Add scraps little and often until the worms have settled in and you're used to the time it takes for them to eat everything up.

5 Cover with a lid, or if you don't have one a piece of old cardboard or newspaper or an old towel will work just as well. It's about keeping the light out and the moisture in. Don't let the wormery dry out, but equally if it gets too wet it will start to smell and the worms can drown. If you do detect an unpleasant odour, either empty the bin (locating your worms and keeping them on one side), wash it and start again or just add more 'brown' material (newspaper, dead leaves, torn-up egg boxes, etc.). If your worms don't seem to be managing the task in hand, your bin might be too dry, in which case empty the material you've added, mix in some 'green' waste (grass cuttings, vegetable peelings, etc.), add a little water and return to the bin.

6 If you can't use your compost straight away, it'll keep perfectly well in sacks in a cool, dry place.

Several **celery** stems and **bay** leaves, to flavour a soup.

....

The last of the **Brussels sprouts**, which I'll blanch and then sauté so I can enjoy them in all their glory as a side veg. I'll give Hal a token sprout, but he's not very keen on them.

Alliums – the edible kind

I've just picked the last leaves from three of the five kale plants, which is good timing because I can lift them and plant onions in their place, as well as in a few other gaps in the borders. I've grown onions in containers before, and they do really well, but I've got space for them in the borders this year and I like the idea of them adding a bit of vertical structure. I urge you to try a few because they pack so much more flavour than shop-bought varieties. Interestingly, it's the sulphur content in the onion that produces their distinctive taste, so give them a feed with a lower potash content for strongly flavoured onions (potash, which refers to soluble salts containing potassium, a component of many fertilisers, prevents them from absorbing sulphur).

I always buy onion sets, or baby onions, as they have a head start once they're in the ground. If the ground is too hard and you're keen to get them going, then plant in large-sized modular trays. You can also start them from seed in trays, but look for smaller packets or share with friends because they don't stay viable for long.

You can plant out your onions up until April, being careful as their leaves are delicate and thin. In the week before you want to plant them out, pop them outside for a few hours each day to 'harden off'. Whether direct-planting or transferring, gently push them into soft soil (enriched with well-rotted organic matter and worked with a fork or trowel before planting) so that the tips are just showing. Give them a bit of space so that the bulbs can develop – 10cm apart is the general rule of thumb – and there's plenty of air circulation around the plants. These can be too much of a temptation for birds once in the ground, so cover them with a bit of netting or set some twigs in a teepee shape over them.

Be prepared that your onions might develop a bit of rust – mine always seem to – which is caused by humidity (hence making sure there's space for airflow). A few yellowish spots are fine, but if it becomes too severe, it's best to lift and remove the plants and stop growing leeks, garlic or onions in the same place for a couple of years. Mildew can also be caused by overcrowding; if your plants show signs of infection, remove the discoloured leaves. Keep an eye out for weeds because the onions have shallow roots and have to compete for moisture. Don't let them dry out, but equally, don't overwater them. It sounds tricky, but little and often (and not at all after rain) is a good guideline.

Know your onions

Spring-planted onions should be ready in late summer or early autumn. Wait for the leaves to die back and then lift, storing in a cool, dry and well-ventilated spot so that the skins can dry. If you're not looking to store them and so don't need tougher skins, harvest as and when you want them. The earlier you pick, the smaller the bulb, but that's not always a bad thing. Autumn-planted onions will be ready in June, so make a note in September to get a few in the ground. Try 'Sturon' and 'Red Baron' in spring, 'Autumn Gold' and 'Shakespeare' in autumn.

Onions need a lot of warmth and light, so if your plot enjoys a limited amount of sunshine (less than nine hours), go for the Japanese varieties, which will cope perfectly well and are bred to overwinter in harsh conditions. Sow in September. Try 'Ishikura' and 'Senshyu'.

Spring onions, or scallions, can be sown from April, planting out every few weeks so you get a continuous crop to liven up your salads. Try 'North Holland Blood Red' and 'White Lisbon'.

Shallots are traditionally planted on the shortest day of the year (21 December) and harvested on the longest (21 June). While I love this connection to the calendar and growing seasons, the reality is that the ground is likely to be too hard in December, so either start off indoors in individual pots in January or, if sowing outdoors, wait until the soil warms, anywhere from the end of February to April, depending in which part of the country you are located. Plant shallot sets as you would onions. Try 'Jermor' and 'Figaro'.

Several **celery** stems, a few sprigs of **thyme** and **bay** for a soup.

Bare-rooted raspberries

As I was cutting back my autumn-fruiting raspberries this morning, I was reminded of a walk Hal and I went on last summer, where we discovered a crop of wild raspberries tangled among the hawthorn that edged the old green lane leading up to an ancient wood. Blackberries and wild strawberries are all part of the foraging spoils you expect to find along a hedgerow, but I had never come across free-range raspberries before. The smaller fruits weren't especially juicy and had a lot of seeds, but that didn't diminish the pleasure of our surprise treat. Our home-grown raspberries are sweet and juicy, and I've managed to ensure that the three varieties I grow provide a crop from July to September (though

not constantly, because we only grow two plants of each type).

Raspberries are an excellent choice when the climate is cold and wet, as they originate in northern Europe. Scotland produces excellent fruits with their mild temperatures and plenty of rain. While they prefer sun, they can also grow well in partial shade, so they're a versatile crop to use in those difficult spots in a small garden – though make sure their position is not too windy because they rely on pollinating insects to fertilise their flowers. However, they don't

do so well in containers, and I have tried! They peak after the first year or two because there isn't enough space for them to put on new growth (canes), which means the harvests becomes rather pitiful. Dwarf varieties are a good compromise, and obviously are ideal for containers. These are widely available; try 'Ruby Beauty' and 'Yummy'.

Raspberry canes (the horticultural name for the plant) are best bought as bare root in winter and this means they're cheaper than pot-grown plants, better for the environment and you'll have more choice when it comes to the varieties on offer. Our raspberry season kicks off with 'Glen Ample', as it produces plenty of large fruits on thornless canes (which is a consideration if you have kids), then comes 'Glen Prosen', which picks up the reins during late summer, and finally 'Autumn Bliss', which copes in a shaded spot and will provide fruit until the first frosts. There are lots of other varieties, even some with gold and black fruits, like 'Golden Everest' and 'Starlight', and there are hybrids that won't rot in heavy, wet soils too.

Plant with about 50cm between each plant and give them a layer of well-rotted manure. Feed each spring with some general-purpose fertiliser and mulch to lock in moisture and suppress weeds.

Bare-rooted raspberries

Depending on whether they're summer- or autumn-fruiting, they need to be treated slightly differently. Once summer varieties have finished fruiting, cut the canes that produced fruit back to the ground and choose around six to eight young canes that have grown in the current season, tying them to supports (either wire running between two posts or trained up a single post), so they can produce fruit next year. February is the time to cut back the canes of autumn varieties, which have just produced fruit, snipping them off at ground level so they can start off again in the spring.

After a few years, you might want to thin the number of canes if they're overcrowded; aim for 10cm gaps between each one. Make sure they don't dry out during hot summer weather and if the fruits appear to discolour and shrivel, you might have an issue with raspberry beetle. Pick off infected fruit, but if the issue continues, an autumn variety might be preferable as they're not so prone to attack. Summer varieties, on the other hand, can be cut back if they're too tall for their supports.

Other bare-root fruit to try

I've had container-grown currants (red, black and white) as well as a gooseberry for several years and have been amazed at how productive these little plants are, especially because they are in the front garden and easily forgotten, especially when it comes to watering.

Like raspberries, these fruits will cope in some shade, performing a useful role in many gardens where sunny spots are quickly filled. They can also be grown as bushes, or as single-stem 'cordons', again a useful characteristic when space is an issue. Apart from regular feeding over winter to early spring, they're fairly low maintenance, though a winter prune to remove old or diseased branches and a summer prune to cut back new growth to two buds to keep their shape will ensure healthy plants.

Try 'Ben Lomond' or 'Ben Sarek' (blackcurrant); 'Rovada' and 'Junifer' (redcurrant); 'Versailles Blanche' (white currant), as well as 'Invicta' or 'Leveller' (gooseberry).

Organic fertilisers

This morning I caught a bit of *English Pastoral: An Inheritance*, on BBC Radio 4. The 2020 book by farmer and author James Rebanks (who wrote the equally brilliant *The Shepherd's Life: A Tale of the Lake District*), it resonates, not because I dream of becoming a farmer with acres to tend, but because, as a grower, I face the same repercussions of using pesticides (same chemicals, different scale) and making too many demands on the soil and surrounding environment. When I think back to my grandparents' gardens (on both sides of the family) their plots were immaculate, with lusciously green lawns and perfectly pest-free shrubs. Though they were very green-fingered, it was the 1970s, and I remember their sheds being packed to the gunnels with a bewildering variety of chemicals – to lay waste and to promote growth.

While James Rebanks writes beautifully, it doesn't change the stark reality that for more than 40 years, modernisation in farming has all but destroyed the health of his fields and livestock: 'A radical experiment', in Rebanks's words, which arguably hasn't had the desired effect. It transpires we've demanded so much from the land that it can no longer support crops and livestock. We are in a vicious circle that requires artificial solutions to provide nutrition and

manage pests because we have stripped the environment of the natural elements that traditionally fuelled this life cycle. According to Rebanks, the use of artificial fertilisers, for both crops and animals, has had a disastrous effect on the environment. Simply put (and I urge you to read his book for a more eloquent and in-depth explanation), in terms of the health of the environment, modern farming is unsustainable. We need to return to the traditional methods of growing crops, raising livestock and caring for the land. We gardeners can do our bit by using natural pest control methods and feeds, in other words, by gardening organically.

Homemade (organic) fertiliser and pest control

There is a wealth of organic alternatives to use to produce healthy, pest-free crops. Even better, they can be made at home using simple store-cupboard ingredients or plants grown in your own garden.

Fertiliser

During the growing season, when plants are using their energies to produce crops, providing additional nutrients helps them remain strong and healthy. It's easy to forget giving them a feed, so I try to do it at the same time each week, for example making it Feed Friday.

COMFREY AND NETTLES Comfrey leaves are rich with nitrogen, phosphorus and potassium (three times as much of the latter as you'll find in farmyard manure). This triumvirate of nutrients is vital for plant health and growth, and makes a nutritious liquid plant feed, or 'tea'.

Russian comfrey is a good variety because it contains high nutrient levels, its leaves can be harvested several times during the growing season and it doesn't produce many seeds, so won't take over a border. Remove the flower stem in the first season to help it bulk up and produce plenty of leaves the following year. To encourage even more leaf growth, if you have grass cuttings or know someone who does, add a few handfuls around the base of the plant every now and then. Alternatively, you could mulch with well-rotted manure.

Comfrey tea

Cut about 1kg of leaves and add to a large bucket of water, let it steep for 4 to 6 weeks and it will produce a marvellous, if unpleasant-smelling, liquid. Alternatively, you can make a concentrate without using water. This is the method I prefer, as it takes up less space and the liquid is less pungent. Simply pack a plastic bottle with leaves, replace the lid and puncture a hole in the top of it. Turn the bottle upside down and hang above a container. As the leaves decay, a highly concentrated liquid will drip out. To use, add about 1-part water to 10-parts concentrate.

Comfrey is considered by some to be too vigorous to grow in a pot, but I've had success growing it in good-sized containers (about 30cm in diameter), which is helpful if you're stuck for space. The plants might not last as long, but if you keep a few self-sown seedlings you can ensure you always have a comfrey plant or two in your garden. It's happy in most soils and likes sunshine. Alternatively, team up with a friend or neighbour to find a disused shared space for it and share the spoils of the liquid fertiliser once it's made. You could also keep an eye out for it growing in the wild.

COFFEE GROUNDS These add nutritional value to the soil, but rather than adding them directly to the soil and plants, which can cause the pH levels to rise, the best way to use them is to add them to home compost. This way, they combine with other organic matter prior to being incorporated into beds or used in containers, and won't introduce acidity to the soil.

BANANAS Bananas are known for their high levels of potassium, which is an essential nutrient for plants. They are also notoriously slow at decomposing and can attract unwanted pests. Try baking banana peel and grinding it down to sprinkle over the soil, or steep peel in a sealed jar for a week or so and use the water to fertilise plants.

CRUSHED EGG SHELLS Egg shells provide calcium, which strengthens a plant's cell structure. The easiest method is to add them directly to the soil, or you can also steep them in boiling water, which will be ready to use a day or two afterwards.

SEAWEED For seaweed, turn to page 34.

WORM CASTS For worm casts, turn to page 70.

Pest control

A healthy garden has a balance of beneficial insects, which are vital to keep pest populations under control. Companion planting (see page 171) is a good strategy to tackle unwelcome visitors, and a variety of organic sprays are effective and won't harm your plot, or the wider environment for that matter, ensuring insects will thrive and crops aren't contaminated with toxic nasties.

GARLIC When I interviewed the head gardener at The Grove, a country house hotel in Wales, he swore by garlic spray. I'm not sure if he still works there, but his garlic legacy certainly lives on for me. He used it as a preventative tonic to reduce infestations of carrot fly and caterpillars, as well as to enhance plant health. Rather than kill pests, its pungent odour makes the plants undesirable as a place to eat or lay eggs. It also won't harm beneficial insects and so helps maintain the balance your garden needs to defend itself.

ORANGES You can use oranges to make a super citrus spray to tackle slugs, aphids, fungus gnats, mealy bugs and ants.

Peel an orange and place the peel into a glass container. Pour 1.2 litres of water over it and allow the solution to sit in a warm spot for 24 hours. Pour the solution through a strainer, removing the peel and saving the citrus-infused water. Add a few drops of castile soap – peppermint-scented castile soap is especially effective. Mix the solution thoroughly to combine. Pour the pesticide into a spray bottle and apply to the leaves.

Garlic spray

Pour 10 litres of water into a large container, then place 400g garlic granules in a muslin bag and tie it to the inside of the container. Leave to infuse, and decant after 24 hours, retaining the granules, which can be reused as long as they emit their garlicky scent. To use, dilute 100ml of the garlic infusion in 10 litres of water in a watering can and sprinkle over the plants. You can also use garlic cloves; about 10 cloves crushed and steeped overnight in 10 litres of water, for a weaker solution that will prevent infestation. Strain to remove the cloves, and apply early morning or evening, when the sun isn't as strong. Store both infusions in the refrigerator for a few days, or in the freezer if you need to store for a longer period.

CHRYSANTHEMUMS These flowers contain a chemical component called pyrethrum, which is capable of paralysing many garden insects.

Pick the flowers of the pyrethrum daisy when they're in full bloom and the 'pyrethrins' in the flower heads are at their peak. Keep the stalks on so you can hang the flowers in a dry, cool and dark place. When brittle, finely grind them in a blender. Combine 100g with 1 litre of water. Boil the mixture for 20 minutes and pour the solution through a strainer. Remove the dried flowers and save the infused water in a spray bottle.

Spray over the entire plant, including the undersides of leaves. Store the solution in the refrigerator for up to two months and keep out of reach from pets and children.

A few **chard** leaves and the last of the **cavolo nero** to make a pesto.

Early spoils

After enough rain for Noah's Ark to set sail, we've finally had a few days of clear blue skies and sunshine. It's amazing the difference it makes to the garden – as if everything has been holding its breath, ready to burst into bud the minute the temperatures rise a little. Spring bulbs are emerging with speed now, and I was surprised to notice that the last two kale plants are sprouting fresh green leaves along their stems and out of their crowns. While I haven't sown new kale plants yet (I'll wait another month or two), this is a welcome way to plug the hunger gap that must be endured in the garden at this in-between time of year (post-harvest and pre-new seedlings). The chard is also putting on fresh

growth and I'm relieved to see that the celery and celeriac, which were left unprotected and had appeared to have succumbed to the frost, have sprung back to life.

It's a good time to weed vegetable beds because the weather is warming the soil and encouraging weeds to germinate. Traditionally vegetables are sown in rows so it's easier to spot rogue weeds, most of which will grow outside these lines, but if, like me, you're sowing to fill gaps, weeds are trickier to spot. If in doubt, let them grow so it's easier to tell the difference.

Spring

Spring sowing (see April 7th).

Chit potatoes and once planted at the end of spring, begin earthing up.

Divide chives if they're in a pot and looking a bit congested.

Plant up pots of thyme, rosemary, mint and tarragon.

Start off perennials like sorrel, asparagus, oca and globe artichokes.

Protect carrots from carrot fly by covering with horticultural fleece.

Pinch out the growing tips of broad beans as soon as beans start to appear at the base of the plant, to reduce the risk of blackfly attack.

Cover strawberry plants with a cloche (recycled, upturned plastic bottles are fine) to encourage early fruit.

Add fresh compost to the soil of patio fruit trees.

Try combining DIY with gardening by creating vertical veg beds or insect hotels.

Add a layer of horticultural fleece to stone-fruit blossoms (plums, apricots, peaches and nectarines) to protect from frost – it's too disheartening to see all that potential ravished by an unwelcome visit.

Hang pheromone traps in apple and plum trees to reduce codling moth.

Regularly check the centre of gooseberry bushes for green gooseberry sawfly caterpillars – they quickly skeletonise leaves if not removed.

Protect soft fruit plants to prevent birds from eating your crop.

Plant sunflowers and teasels to provide seeds snacks later in the year for winter wildlife.

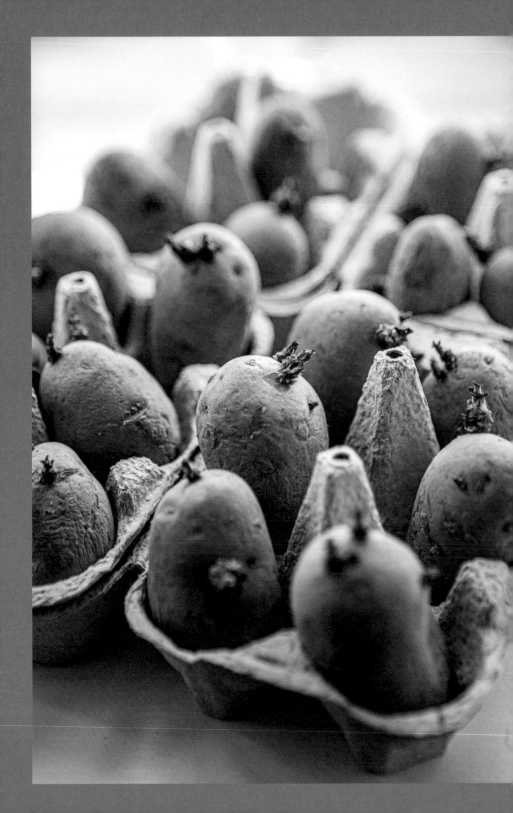

Potatoes

I've just ordered a 1kg bag of Charlotte new potatoes – there isn't room to grow them in my garden, but my mum, who has a good-sized veg plot, grows enough for both our families. I have grown them in containers and heavy-duty bags and have been happy with the results, but I'm pleased to be able to use the space for other crops this year, especially as I will still have home-grown spuds to enjoy. New potatoes are a type of potato referred to as first early or second early – they can be started in February, but in our case, it's better late than never! Essentially first and second earlies are fast growers (ready 10 weeks after planting) and tend to cost more when they hit the shops in June, so are often the spud of choice for a veg patch or allotment. They also taste far better eaten super fresh, which is another reason to try growing them at home. Maincrop (meaning the principal crop of the season) potatoes are the larger varieties, and these are best suited to baking or roasting and, for that matter, growing in the ground. You can try growing them in bags and large pots, but ideally the more space you can give them the better the harvest, which is approximately 20 weeks after planting in March or April (traditionalists take note: to some, March 17th, or St Patrick's Day, is *the* day to plant potatoes, whereas for others it's all about waiting for the first dandelion to bloom before planting).

It's fascinating to think that potatoes are an ancient vegetable, in the true sense of the word. The earliest recorded trace of the spud was found in the Peruvian Andes at around 6000 BC. I love the idea that, 5,000 years later, the Inca civilisation relied so much on them that time was measured by how long it took to cook a potato. Sadly, the cultivation of potatoes on a global scale doesn't give rise to such a charming anecdote: According to American author and journalist, Charles C. Mann, potatoes 'set the template for modern agriculture – the so-called agro-industrial complex'. In his book *1493: Uncovering the New World Columbus Created*, he concludes that the introduction of the potato also brought with it the first intensive fertiliser – Peruvian guano – as well as the first artificial pesticide, a form of arsenic used to tackle the Colorado potato beetle, which ultimately formed the basis of the modern pesticide industry. Spoiler alert: it was these new techniques and farming practices which seemed so exciting and revolutionary in the 1940s and 1950s that they eventually resulted in what critics call the 'toxic treadmill', where chemical pest controls are continually upgraded at an alarming rate in an effort to keep one step ahead of the pests, who inevitably continue to adapt, thrive and essentially outwit the scientists.

To chit or not to chit?

Seed potatoes (potatoes from which new sprouts will grow) benefit from a bit of encouragement before they're even planted, which involves putting them somewhere cool and light until a few shoots appear ready to, well, hit the ground running. This is done by a technique called chitting (the word chit is old English, meaning 'a shoot'). Basically, you're putting your Safe-Haven-Certified seed potatoes, bought from a reputable garden centre or specialist grower (not leftover spuds, which might have been treated to prevent sprouting and be more prone to disease), the end with the most eyes facing up, somewhere not too sunny but with plenty of light, so a windowsill in a cool room is ideal. To keep things looking neat and to ensure they're not mistaken for stray supper ingredients, pop the tubers in an egg box (this also ensures they don't touch, which is important). Don't worry if they start to wrinkle; signs of ageing, as with life in general, are absolutely natural because by exposing them to light and a bit of warmth, you're speeding up the growing process.

The jury's out as to whether chitting is necessary or not, apart from the obvious benefit of getting on and doing something. Don't underestimate its appeal to children too, if that's a consideration in your household. All sorts of fun can be had, from pimping up the egg carton to keeping a growth chart that measures the shoots while at the same time encouraging a healthy enthusiasm for basic maths.

There are plenty of growers (among them commercial, but then again, would they have enough egg boxes and space to lovingly chit millions of spuds?) who find this an unnecessary task, but since growers for centuries have done it, I think there's some benefit. There is also a practical application behind the idea: Planting pre-sprouted potatoes saves around 10–14 days in the growing cycle, which is a consideration for those living in regions where the spring gets going quickly and the summer can be short-lived. Getting a head start will ensure varieties that take longer to mature (more than 20 weeks) can reach their peak and provide a larger yield. It also means that you get an earlier crop too. You're looking for about three sprouts per potato – more than that and it will encourage too many roots, so remove any that are unwanted. If your taters are large and have produced an abundance of sprouts, cut them into chunks with about three sprouts per piece – adopting a thrifty approach should never be frowned upon in gardening, and it means you can share your spoils with anyone else who is looking forward to eating home-grown potatoes. Let them 'heal' or dry out before planting (a few days should do the trick), but if you're impatient to get planting, you can dip the cut ends in wood ash.

Start chitting about four weeks before you plan to plant them out, but hang back if an unexpected frost is predicted. The sprouts will ideally be about 5cm long before planting.

How to grow

Container-grown potatoes are a great compromise when space is a consideration – though if you do have room to grow them in the ground they'll not only provide a crop but will also clear weedy ground (the dense foliage blocks out the light) and help break up the soil while they're at it. The principle is essentially the same whether they're in a pot or a border. Start by filling a container about one-third full with soil or digging a trench about 20cm deep. Plant about three or four seed potatoes in a pot or at about 10cm intervals in the ground. Cover with around 10–15cm of soil and wait for roughly 20cm of growth to appear before adding another layer of compost, enough to bury about half of the growing stem (otherwise called earthing up). This helps to protect the tubers and keep them cool, which is important as they taste bitter if exposed to excessive heat. Repeat every three weeks until they flower, and be sure to water containers regularly. Harvest about two to three weeks later, when the flowers fade.

Christmas spuds

If you're planting new potatoes, why not keep four or five back to plant in August? Store in a cool, dark place away from onions, apples and bananas, which emit ethylene gas that encourages sprouting. Quick-maturing varieties like 'Rocket' and 'Swift' are perfect for large pots or bags, which can be brought indoors before the first frosts, to continue growing in a greenhouse, garage or porch.

(Not so dear) Old Blighty

Potato blight can be an issue. It is easy to spot, as dark brown spots appear on the leaves and stems until the plant collapses entirely. One of the most effective ways to cope with this fungal disease is to make sure you grow them in a different spot each year on a four-year rotation, which prevents the disease from infecting the crop the following year. Providing good ventilation also helps, as it prevents the spores from settling, so make sure to give your spuds as much room as possible so that air can circulate. In a small city garden, it might be more sensible to grow them in large sacks or bags and change the soil each year. Try disease-resistant varieties if you're especially worried, and as the fungus thrives in humid conditions, water at the base of the plants in the mornings; this allows any moisture on the leaves to evaporate during the day. If blight appears, dig up and destroy the entire plant and all the potatoes.

Cloches, cold frames and plastic bottles

I couldn't afford a greenhouse when I moved into my first garden flat. I was working as the staff writer for BBC *Gardeners' World Magazine* and responsible for their craft-based 'Fresh Ideas' section. I am the first to admit that DIY isn't one of my strengths (I lack the necessary attention to detail), and I remember it being rather stressful. However, there was a silver lining of sorts, and I was allowed to keep the things I made, assuming they hadn't fallen apart by the end of the photographic shoot. My allotment plot featured a salmon-pink bike-wheel bird-scarer, I had a nifty wooden box in which to store seeds in my office, and a rather overambitious MDF cube seat in my garden, which I had attempted to cover in mosaic tiles (it's much harder than it looks and I only had time to complete three sides on the day of the shoot). My most prized 'make' was a simple cold frame: a brick structure (only four bricks high, so no need for cement) on top of which I had fixed half an Edwardian sash window I had salvaged from a skip. It turned out to be a really useful addition to my garden and, depending on the time of year, was filled with seedlings, cuttings or tender plants.

While I was lucky to be able to spare a bit of space for the cold frame (just a metre by half a metre), I realise this isn't an option for everyone. The good news is that you can create smaller versions, or cloches, by using upturned recycled plastic bottles to cover individual seedlings in pots or in the ground – cut off the bottom of the bottle and leave the cap on to use as ventilation. If you can get your hands on an old water-cooler bottle, all the better, as its larger circumference is more likely to sit on top of a container or cover several seedlings at once. There are also made-for-purpose cloches available in the shops or online, to suit a wide range of budgets.

Essentially, cold frames and cloches provide protection from frost, wind and rain, and if on the ground, the glass or plastic covering helps raise the temperature of the soil. (Inside a cold frame structure it is usually about 5–10°C warmer than the outside environment.) Ideally they should be south-facing, though this isn't always possible or even necessary with smaller cloches, or if you're looking to use them for

cuttings, which require a shady, rather than sunny, spot. However, it's important that they're easy to get to, so you can keep an eye on your plants, making sure they're not getting too hot, suffering from high moisture levels (in which case, prop open for a few hours to encourage good ventilation), or are vulnerable to slugs, greenfly or other pests.

Making your own mini cold frame ...

Build a solid structure for the base, using wood, bricks or even straw bales, making sure it can withstand the wind. If you can't get your hands on a recycled window, use a sheet of glass or polycarbonate and secure it to a wooden frame, adding a handle, which can be useful.

History of cloches

The idea of protecting plants dates back to nineteenth-century French market gardens, where rows of vegetable seedlings were protected with cloches – the French word for bell. Imagine how chic that must have looked? Essentially portable mini greenhouses, they were soon replaced by cheap polythene covers, to cope with the modern demands of agriculture.

Cold frames, or cucumber frames, as they were known in English Victorian gardens, were considered too fragile, so the industrious Victorians reinforced the design, creating a cast-iron frame. They were groundbreaking, too, as for many, the idea of growing Mediterranean summer vegetables – which required a greenhouse or a walled garden, not to mention a team of gardeners – was simply out of reach. The introduction of cast-iron cucumber frames meant that by the late nineteenth century most families could own one or two and take advantage of their more favourable growing conditions.

To retain as much warmth from the sun as possible, try painting the inside white, or even lining it with aluminium foil. You can fill a black bucket with water and place it inside the frame during the day where it will gather heat, and then release it during the night.

… or cloche

Though small, cloches are still a gardener's best friend, offering seedlings much-needed protection against the elements as well as unwelcome diners like birds and rabbits. I also find them a useful buffer that prevents seedlings from being accidentally trampled over when my dog Teddy takes a wander through the veg beds. Essentially, the transparent cover is the key feature, allowing sun rays through it to warm the soil, whether in the ground or in a pot. Warmth helps seeds get off to a flying start, and in theory, establishes a healthy, strong plant that will provide a bumper crop later on in the season.

Wire-frame hanging baskets are a cheap and easy way to make a cloche and come in different sizes, depending on the amount of seeds you'll be sowing.

1. Turn the wire-frame basket dome-side up and attach a layer of double-sided sticky tape to the edge.

2. Cover the entire wire-frame basket with secondary glazing film and attach to the sticky tape. Leave an additional 5cm border of film beyond the tape edge.

3. Use a hairdryer to shrink the film to a tight fit and cut off any excess. (While the film lasts a few months, you can replace it and repair it with more film, should the elements take their toll.)

4. About two weeks before sowing, position the cloche over the area of soil where seed will be sown to warm the soil. Remove the basket to sow seeds and then re-cover to provide protection as seeds germinate and start to grow.

5. Remove the cloche once seedlings are well-established or are touching the cloche, to avoid problems with disease or damaged plants.

How to use a cold frame or cloche ...

... in Spring

Ideal for hardening young plants in pots, in other words, acclimatising them to the harsher weather conditions before it's time to plant them outside.

... in Summer

Provides plants like tomatoes and chillies with more heat before the season actually starts, helping to speed up their growth, as well as creating a nurturing environment for cuttings.

... in Autumn

Extend your harvest season by at least four weeks and protect young plants and cuttings from dropping temperatures. Keep it clear from fallen leaves and branches.

... in Winter

Overwinter plants, ready for the spring, with the option of caring for tender varieties by adding a layer of extra protection (bubble plastic on the inside, for example), though bear in mind, this will reduce the light and ventilation as well, especially in the snow.

Winter crops to start off in a cold frame or under a cloche

Beetroot	Broccoli	Cabbage
Carrots	Chard	Kale
Lettuce	Radish	Spinach
Tomatoes		

Five **chestnut mushrooms** and a few **pea shoots** for a risotto.

Choosing varieties

In his book *An Ear To The Ground: Understanding Your Garden,*
Ken Thompson, author and botanist, makes the case for growing blackcurrants in preference to blueberries, largely because they're much higher
in antioxidants and easier to grow (blackcurrants don't require acidic
ericaceous soil). The book is an inspirational read because Ken is able to
convey complex scientific information simply, allowing you to connect
with your own patch and, perhaps more importantly, understand what
is going on in it. Whether you agree with him on the blackcurrants or
not (it's literally a matter of taste), he raises an excellent point about carefully considering which type of crop to grow. When space is an issue (not
to mention, budget, time and experience), being pragmatic about what
you're going to try will make a huge difference to your experience and
results. Sure, blueberries are delicious, and it's not a huge undertaking to
buy a bag of ericaceous compost to fill a container, but if it's a question of
growing a blueberry *or* blackcurrant, it's worth weighing up whether one
might have the edge for various reasons.

Don't get me wrong, I'm not suggesting that every crop requires a
careful evaluation of its pros and cons (though that's not a *terrible* idea if
you have a small garden) – at some point every growing season, I'll find
myself in a garden centre surrounded by rows of plugs and my shopping
list goes out the window and I impulsively buy varieties that hadn't even
made it onto the 'maybe' wish list. This is all part of the fun of growing
your own, but it can be equally satisfying to show a bit of restraint and
search websites and garden centre benches for a particular crop, or
variety, that ticks all your boxes.

Once you've drawn up a wish list of crops – mine usually comes in at around 65 varieties before I have to ruthlessly cull it – you can start to whittle out the ones that won't do well in your particular location (too sunny, or too shady, etc.). Next comes its growing habitat – if you only have room to fill one border with crops, you'll have to prioritise from the types that won't appreciate being grown in containers (asparagus, millet and raspberries, for example), or vice versa if you don't have veg beds, you'll have to choose the crops that like their leg room to be snug. Disease resistance is another consideration, and a good idea for new growers, because the more success you have with the whole process – from sowing or growing to harvesting – the more you'll want to continue and the more experience you can gain. And besides, even the most experienced gardeners would prefer not to have to battle with pests and diseases if they can help it – though perhaps if it came with the promise of flavour, they'd be prepared to wage a green-fingered war.

Next, you can choose based on flavour and the crop itself. There's nothing like reading the descriptions in the catalogues, and I often find that my wish list grows again at this point, as I can't resist a tomato with a sweet, honey flavour or a nutty-tasting kalette (a cross between kale and Brussels sprouts).

Heirloom varieties

Over the years, I've been drawn towards heirloom varieties (or old-fashioned fruit and veg) – an old cultivar of a plant or crop, the types often left behind in the scramble to breed faultless hybrid varieties. Yet these historic varieties, which are often specific to a region, having thrived for years in the climate and soil of that area, possess qualities that we are once again looking for in our food. For me, flavour will always have the edge over the characteristics that have been intensely bred out of the variety in order to achieve hardiness, disease resistance, higher yield, uniformity or novelty-factor. In the end, a bland, mushy tomato is a huge disappointment after a summer of care and expectation, whereas the smoky sweetness of an heirloom tomato, even if it has needed a little extra nurturing, is something to be celebrated.

Ken Thompson argues that it isn't just the flavour that is lost in the effort to produce perfect crops; nutritional value is also compromised. Modern breeders are understandably excited by hybridisation, but this comes at a price. Modern roses are a good example; they look beautiful and reliably produce bloom after bloom, but with little or no fragrance. One could argue, what's a rose without its heady scent?

This echoes James Rebanks's lament about modern farming in his book *English Pastoral: An Inheritance*, because Thompson maintains it is selective breeding, as well as the reliance on chemical fertilisers, which means that crops contain a diluted concentration of vitamins

and minerals. My understanding is that by choosing heritage varieties and growing them in a chemical-free compost using organic feed, these issues can be avoided. In other words, not only will the crops you grow taste delicious, but they'll also be better for you.

Be adventurous too...

While growing familiar crops is always a good place to start, especially if you need to be pragmatic about what you can and can't grow, don't under-estimate the thrill of trying something completely new. One of the things I love most about devouring the seed catalogues is finding the weird and wonderful varieties. The walking stick cabbage (or giant Jersey kale) was my first foray into stranger things, which I grew in the over-filled borders of my first London flat. I couldn't resist it when I saw the pictures in the seed catalogue (imagine a cross between a very tall aeonium – the likes of which you would see growing in Cornwall and further south on the Isles of Scilly – and an elongated Brussels sprout, and you're about there). Although it's technically a biennial, meaning it germinates and grows in its first year, blooms, sets seeds and dies in its second, it's best to harvest the edible leaves in the first year (which were traditionally wrapped

around loaves of bread to protect them from the old ovens and impart a distinctive flavour). As its name suggests, the single stem can be varnished or stained and used as a walking stick. In fact, in their native Channel Islands they were grown for this purpose, with leaves removed to feed to livestock and prevent the stem from twisting. Don't ask me why, but I didn't get around to making a walking stick, and writing about them now has inspired me to grow them again, especially as Hal collects walking sticks. As it's single-stemmed, it'll grow up and out of the border, so won't take up too much room. Bees and butterflies go wild for the nectar, too, so while it might be a bit of an oddball, it has plenty to offer ... including a gift for the rambler in your life.

Martin Crawford's timeless classic *How to Grow Perennial Vegetables* is not only an excellent guide to growing vegetables but also throws up some unexpected varieties. The founder of the Agroforestry Research Trust (which studies the results of growing both trees and agricultural/horticultural crops on the same piece of land), Martin is the leading expert on perennial veg (plants that produce a crop year after year), and his book includes some quite unexpected treats, such as daffodil garlic and ostrich ferns, the latter of which come up early in the spring and can be prepared like asparagus. For years he has been urging us to consider this group of vegetables for a number of good reasons. Saving time maintaining the veg patch is the obvious advantage, as keeping the same crop in the same spot calls for less weeding, digging and mulching throughout the year and come next spring, there's no need to sow seed again in that particular bit of the garden. There's also an environmental consideration for giving them a go: these crops are low-maintenance and therefore a low-carbon alternative to annual varieties.

So why is it taking so long for the collective penny to drop when it comes to perennial veg? While I don't have the answer, I think it makes sense to give these crops a try, especially as extreme summer weather (too wet, too hot, too windy) as well as not having enough time to get outside can result in an underproductive plot. Growing perennial veg could be the answer: Choosing varieties that will grow back every year, are more robust and require much less care than annuals will make a positive impact on gardening morale as well as your larder. It's a win-win proposition, and here are some I'd recommend...

Sorrel

A great alternative to spinach, you can eat the young, succulent leaves in salads, as well as using the larger, tougher leaves to make a delicious soup. One of the earliest crops to start in spring, it has a tangy flavour.

Red-veined sorrel is a beautiful addition to both the veg patch and the plate, but there's something just as tempting about the common broad-leaved variety too, with its vibrant green colour. All varieties prefer a bit of shade, and they will need watering in a long hot spell, otherwise they will run to seed. Sow seeds from March to May, thinning seedlings out to about 30cm apart to give them plenty of room as they bulk up over the years, but you can always thin to 10cm and then dig up any clumps that are getting too restricted in years to come and either give to friends or plant elsewhere to increase your own stocks of sorrel. You will need a few plants if you're cooking it, as it reduces down a lot.

Asparagus

Once you've harvested your first spears you'll wonder why you didn't try growing it before. It's a short-seasoned crop that really is best eaten fresh, but what could be more decadent than harvesting this expensive-to-buy crop from your own plot? A well-known restauranteur once told me a lovely story about a friend who adored asparagus but was incredibly particular about its freshness. Each April, he would take a small camping stove and a saucepan of water to his asparagus patch. He'd set up the stove at the end of a row and wait for the water to boil. Once ready, he'd dash off to cut some spears and sprint back to immediately plunge them into the boiling water, to then eat a few minutes later. How's that for freshly harvested! Ironically, you do need to show a bit of patience before you can harvest your first spears, giving them three years to get established. The good news is that you can speed the process up and buy two-year-old corms (bulb-like sections of the parent-plant's stem, from which new plants can grow). This enables you to enjoy a modest-sized snack after the first growing season with the promise of much more to come the following year.

Choose a sunny spot but don't worry too much about the soil type. Plant out in March, placing the 'crowns' on a peak-shaped trench (think an upturned V), covering the roots with soil and leaving the bud tips just showing. 'Backlim' and 'Gijnlim' are recommended by the RHS and are widely available. For something a little more unusual, go for 'Ariane' and 'Stewart's Purple'.

Globe artichoke

A great choice for the veg patch if, like me, your enthusiasm for this delectable vegetable is put to the test when you get it into the kitchen (unless you're an adept cook or professional chef, it's a complete faff to prepare artichokes). As the plant is wonderfully architectural (growing up to 1.5m), with silvery-green leaves and large purple flowers, it easily earns its keep in the garden if you don't get to harvest it. However, if you're game, pick the buds when they're the size of golf balls from July onwards, and keep an eye out for a second flush later in the summer. If left, the flowers last well into autumn, providing a welcome seed supply for hungry birds during the winter. The best varieties to go for are 'Green Globe' and 'Violetta di Chioggia'. Sow seeds in now (and up to April) either directly in the soil or in seed trays, or you can buy young plants from garden centres. Water if there's a dry spell or feed in the spring with a general fertiliser. It's a good idea to protect plants during winter by covering them with straw or well-rotted manure.

Egyptian walking onion

This crop will amaze your friends because the plants quite literally walk through your vegetable patch. OK, perhaps it's more of a topple on closer inspection, but they look fantastic and it's quite fun to have a crop start in one area of your veg bed and end up in another, without any help. The reason for their name is that they produce a cluster of little bulbs at the tip of the plant. These bulbs develop roots when they mature and, because they're only supported on a thin, chive-like stem, they fall over. Once the bulb cluster hits the soil, it roots and begins to grow and so the process continues. They appear very early on in spring, enlivening home-cooked dishes with fresh flavour. You can plant them all year round.

Horseradish

If you don't have oodles of space to let it romp away, this one might be a good idea as a container crop. Just find a sunny spot in well-drained soil (or add a few handfuls of horticultural grit if you're planting in pots) and horseradish plants will happily thrive year after year. It's hard to find seed, so plant root cuttings from March to May at about 30cm deep and on an angle. By October it'll be ready for harvesting. Try to pick little and often to enjoy young, tender roots – you can store horseradish in your fridge for up to three months. It's thought that the roots taste the very best after frosts – so if you can wait until you see leaves die back, all the better. Freshly grated or made into a sauce, it's delicious with beef and mackerel, and there are plenty of recipe ideas to be found online in gardening and lifestyle magazine blogs.

Oca

I haven't grown oca yet and am looking forward to giving it a try. It looks truly beautiful – somewhere between a small, knobbly Jerusalem artichoke and a new potato, but with a pink blush skin. It's said to have the same waxy texture as a potato and a delicious lemony aftertaste. Plant tubers in the ground in late May when the soil has warmed up, and mulch with a layer of well-rotted compost to help retain moisture during the summer months. They're a great alternative to potatoes because they don't suffer from blight, which causes growers no end of angst, obliterating potato and tomato crops almost overnight. Perfect for December harvests, this little tuber can be eaten raw or boiled and smothered with butter – perhaps something new to try for this year's Christmas lunch to impress your family?

Skirret

This is an old-fashioned variety of root vegetable that was widely grown when men wore togas and spuds were yet to be introduced to the UK. Thanks to the renaissance of growing your own and the interest in heritage varieties, skirret is making something of a comeback – though I expect most of us would need to double-check in a seed catalogue before we could describe it to a fellow grower, and a specialist catalogue at that. Sow seed in pots in early spring, leaving in a cold frame or with a little protection, potting on as needs be and planting out in the summer. It's worth tracking down as it provides a double harvest – the shoots can be picked in spring and taste delicious simply tossed in butter and garlic, while the clusters of long white roots can be harvested in autumn (preferably after a light frost to improve its flavour) and cooked just as you would a parsnip. It's a hardy vegetable too, so you really can plant and then pretty much forget about it until you want to eat it. It likes moisture though, so cover with mulch and do water if it's a hot, dry summer to prevent the roots from going too woody.

Jerusalem artichoke

In the past, these edible tubers have earned their keep on my allotment as a windbreak, thanks to their tall foliage. In a smaller garden I think they would work well at the back of a border next to a fence to act as a screen, or in large pots to help contain them as they will spread over time. Plant them fairly deep, about 10–15cm, and leave about 30cm between each tuber. As they can grow more than 2m in height, once they've reached 30–40cm, earth up the soil (as you do with potatoes) to anchor them in the ground and prevent them from rocking too much in the wind, and if necessary, stake them too. If you don't want them to get too tall, cut them back in summer to about 1.5m. Once the leaves turn yellow in autumn, prune the stems back down to the stumps. A good trick is to lay these prunings over the plants to keep the soil warm and make life a bit easier when it comes to harvesting the tubers if it's frosty during late autumn and winter. Lift carefully with a fork, leaving some tubers in the ground to come back in spring. They have an utterly delicious nutty flavour, however, it would be unfair of me not to point out that, because they contain a carbohydrate that isn't broken down during digestion, they can cause wind. I've been reassured by a chef that making them into a soup solves this problem, but I say throw caution to the, ahem, wind, and enjoy them roasted and mashed with potato on top of fish pie too. Another chef's tip is to go for smooth-skinned varieties like 'Fuseau' or 'Dwarf Sunray' as it saves time preparing the otherwise knobbly varieties.

Sea kale

In recent travels where I've been lucky enough to interview some of our most brilliant gardeners and chefs, I've learnt that home-grown sea kale is quite different to the wild crop found on sand dunes. No matter how growers have attempted to recreate that salt-laden atmosphere (the brilliant head gardener at The Pig Hotel has even dutifully sprayed his crops with salt water, to little or no effect), it produces a more subtle flavour grown inland. However, this doesn't mean it's not worth growing – it's a tasty crop that, like rhubarb, can be forced to produce an early, more tender crop with a pale appearance, which looks very pretty on a plate. It's an easy technique that calls for a bin, bucket or – if you'd like to be more stylish – a terracotta forcer, which you put over the plant to completely block out the light (see page 262).

Unbelievably, one of the main reasons this native crop is now regarded as unusual is because the Victorians loved it so much, they almost ate it to extinction. Given its natural habitat, sandy, free-draining soil is ideal, but you can always add horticultural grit to loamy or heavier soil to recreate these conditions. Either sow seed in April to June (soak it for a day prior to sowing) and harvest in late summer, or if you'd like to try forcing seed-sown crops, it's advised to wait until the winter of the third growing season. Alternatively you can buy 'thongs', or bare-roots to you and me, to plant in spring, ready to force the following January. Eat the stems raw, boiled or steamed and enjoy its smoky, buttery flavour.

Nothing to harvest this week. This time next year, I plan
to fill this 'hungry gap' with late-summer-planted **leeks** and
sprouting broccoli, which will overwinter and provide
a welcome spring harvest.

Vertical veg

I am in two minds about the concept of vertical growing. Social media is awash with beautiful images of sumptuous green walls from all over the world. The sight of lush green foliage springing out from exterior and interior walls of city buildings is becoming increasingly common, and garden designers regularly incorporate them into their show gardens, creating intricate plant tapestries that hang in the garden like works of art. I have no doubt that green walls (and roofs, for that matter) are clever solutions that can help combat the climate change crisis by reducing the carbon footprint of a building by making it more energy efficient, which leads to a decrease in carbon emissions. (There's evidence to suggest they mitigate the urban heat island effect, absorb and filter stormwater, reduce pollution and act as carbon sinks too.) They also improve our sense of well-being in inner cities and make the most of all potential growing spaces. The impact they have on our environment is truly exciting, but for the home grower, this way of growing is hard to sustain, and achieving a lush, green shagpile-carpet effect is a challenge when budget *is* an issue and the green wall is required to last for a growing season and beyond. Over the last

10 years, improvements have been made to the pocket-sized containers that are sold to help gardeners get the green-wall look, but nevertheless, like the small, gimmicky tin cans and children's welly containers, their size ultimately poses some issues – namely providing enough soil and nutrients in which to grow plants, as well as supplying and retaining enough moisture so plants don't dry out and become stressed. As with all small pots, there are plants that will cope in these conditions better than others: Mediterranean herbs, which don't mind poor, dry soil, or lettuce, which doesn't have an extensive root system (though the latter still requires regular watering to prevent the leaves from tasting bitter). If you're buying these kits, be prepared to do your research and budget for a watering system, which will dramatically improve the results.

Even if space and watering considerations rule out a green wall, there are plenty of ways to utilise the vertical space in your garden or on your balcony, which I'm willing to bet will be underused otherwise.

Choosing trailing crops that can be trained up and over things, like pumpkin and squashes (see page 168) is an easy option – whether using an existing support, like an arch or an arbour, or constructing a

teepee or trellis. Not only are you maximising space but they'll also be creating shade under their leaf canopy as they grow, which could be utilised for crops that need a bit of protection. However, this could also cast unwanted shadows, so consider the position carefully.

Tumbling tomatoes, strawberries and outdoor varieties of cucumber can be grown in hanging baskets or upcycled alternatives (colanders work well here as they provide drainage and can be lined with hessian to help retain the soil).

Guttering can be fixed to the wall at intervals – as you would a shelf – to create tiers in which you can grow herbs and salad crops, and multi-level raised beds, which look like stairs, provide a great surface area for soil while taking up a smaller footprint than if they were laid out on the ground side by side.

Shed, garage, greenhouse and other flat roofs are often overlooked as a possible growing space, but they have lots of potential. If they're too high off the ground, access can be an issue, but when space is at a premium, any area that provides a platform for containers or raised beds is worth considering. I have toyed with the idea of levelling my shallow, sloping potting shed roof to provide a small bed for salads and herbs, but sadly I think the neighbourhood cats, who aren't brave enough to visit our garden because of our dog, Teddy, might take their revenge by using this out-of-reach soil pit as a loo.

Make your own green wall using old pallets

Upcycling an old pallet makes an effective green wall and can be a cheaper alternative to shop-bought versions.

1 Take a pallet and on one side, remove planks of wood in sets of two, leaving the first in place at the 'bottom' of the pallet. You're looking to create three planting troughs – one at the bottom, one in the middle and one at the top – with the planks of wood you're left with. A claw hammer should be fine to ease the wood away from the frame, but it might be easier with a crowbar.

2 Line these three troughs with plastic – old compost bags are ideal. Use an upholstery staple gun to attach the plastic to the inside of the trough. Staple the plastic about 2cm from the top of the trough so that when you fill it with soil, you'll cover up the plastic lining.

3 Carefully pierce the bottom of the plastic liners to provide some drainage and then fill with compost.

4 Choose a sunny spot and hang the pallet on a wall with appropriate attachments. Alternatively you can lean it up against a wall or shed, but make sure it's at a bit of angle to reduce the risk of it toppling over.

5 Plant in situ, as you would if you were planting in a container, adding water-retaining granules to help retain moisture, and continue to water regularly so that the soil doesn't dry out. Also, be diligent when it comes to regular feeding.

Wild garlic (buzz up with salt and oil to drizzle over the top of pizzas) and **nettles** for a tasty fruity tea (just add boiling water).

....

Savoy cabbage. Though small, when shredded this will provide some greens for a couple of meals if combined with other greens.

Zero-waste food

Reading Cecil Henry Middleton's 1937 book, *From Garden to Kitchen*, reminds me that there probably isn't anything new under the sun. One of the first celebrity gardeners, who passionately supported the government's campaign to 'Dig for Victory' during the Second World War, he writes that 'Many of us may live to see the roots (or the tops) of the dock and thistle dished up on our dining tables'.

While Middleton was a bit of a revolutionary when it came to food consumption, the same can't be said for his attitude towards women: the full title of his book reads *From Garden to Kitchen: Wherein the gardener learns how to grow vegetables and the housewife how to cook them*. That said, I like the fact that he makes the connection between gardener and chef, produce and taste. He and the co-author, food writer and broadcaster Ambrose Heath, take you on a charming ramble through the veg garden and provide a fascinating insight into the relationship between gardener and chef in pre-Second World War Britain. They also make the point, which might seem obvious to some, that all vegetable plants originated in wild weeds and were hybridised by gardeners to yield delectable produce.

The catchy slogan 'zero waste' made me assume that this approach was a modern solution to the problem of consumerism. It turns out it is a rebranding of the more prosaic attitude towards life, when food is scarce and household items expensive. If you can only afford a bunch of carrots, necessity and thrift dictates you'll consume the entire plant – roots and tips. (The same can be said for meat, and the 'nose-to-tail' approach.)

Today, *zero waste* is a catch-all term that can be applied to every aspect of our lifestyle. It's a burgeoning movement in response to the ever-increasing need to reduce our waste, from plastics floating in the oceans to mountains of food waste. Our unwanted 'stuff' ends up in landfill, creating methane, a gas that contributes to climate change, or is consigned to incinerators that produce other noxious fumes. In the 1990s, zero waste emerged as a concept for total recycling, and in 2002 the Zero Waste International Alliance was formed, an organisation of scientists and waste-management experts that is working towards a world without waste.

Living sustainably and keeping the environment at the forefront of our minds can be daunting, and in some cases unrealistic. It's best to approach this with small steps, and trying zero waste from a veg-growing point of view is a great way to start your journey. While the action might feel insignificant, it all helps.

The first thing to consider is what you are using in your garden – reusing and recycling potential plant containers rather than buying in plastic ones, sharing deliveries of compost with neighbours to reduce the number of bags and journeys needed and using foraged hazel sticks for bean teepees rather than buying bamboo alternatives are all ways to garden in a zero-waste way. If you're growing your own crops, you'll not only be reducing food waste, you'll also potentially be creating new plants and the nutrients those plants will need. For example, you'll pick a handful of fresh tomatoes off the vine to use in a salad rather than a boxful (where the last few turn mouldy and need to be thrown in the food bin). When you eat the tomatoes, you can also save the seeds from a couple of fruits, ready to grow next year. I'm even experimenting with using the leaves in scented candles. But even if you're not doing that, the spent plant can go on the compost heap to help nourish the soil next year.

Zero waste is particularly interesting if you're growing in a small garden – if you're restricted by how much space you have to grow, why wouldn't you want to be able to make the most of your crops, both in terms of what you eat and what can be regrown? There are lots of vegetables that will provide a second, albeit slightly different, harvest. Beetroot, for example, grow a second flush of leaves from just the end tip, which, like the first leaves, can be added to salad or used to make a tasty

pesto. Other roots from whose tips edible leaves can be grown include parsnips, radish, turnips, sweet potatoes and yams. Celery can also be regrown, as long as the 'growing tip', which is within the stalks, remains intact. Similarly, there are also rhizomes, like ginger, which can be cut into sections and planted in a pot of soil. After a few months, the small piece of rhizome will have grown (there will be leaves above the soil) and is ready to harvest – some to eat and some to regrow. It's the same principle for turmeric, though it will take longer to produce new edible roots. Leeks will also regrow if you plant the rooted stem – they can even be regrown indoors using water rather than soil! It's a fascinating subject, and one that might appeal to kids too, and there are lots of great websites and books to explore – I've recommended a few on the resources list on page 283.

Soil, worms and other wonders

Today seems as good a day as any to draw your attention to the soil in your garden – whether it's in borders or containers, the same rules apply. I've covered the wonderful work that worms do to improve soil, but in this entry, I'm focusing on how to make compost from grass cuttings, prunings and other unwanted organic matter from the garden, as well as compostable food waste. Queen of Herbs (as Jamie Oliver quite rightly named her) Jekka McVicar believes that 'The soil is the engine of your plot'. I've used this quote countless times, but as she is such a well-

respected grower, with so much experience, I wouldn't dream of trying to improve this statement. Essentially, Jekka is saying that if the soil is packed with nutrients, like a steam engine's coal-filled furnace when the train needs to pick up speed, it will provide exactly what your plants need to produce a bumper crop at harvest time.

It's staggering to think that in one tiny teaspoon of soil there are, quite literally, billions of microorganisms, which play a part in the soil's life cycle, alongside worms

and insects, of course. These microorganisms are hard at work, breaking down plant matter and animal tissue, creating airways and introducing nutrients, which ensure plants can access air, water and nutrients. Once you understand this, it makes sense that replenishing the organic matter upon which these vital microorganisms feed and thrive is an essential responsibility for us growers. Think of it like a drink of squash – when you have a bit left in the bottom of the glass, you'll need to add more concentrate as well as water, otherwise the mixture will be very weak, with only the merest hint of flavour.

Soil ...

If you're waiting for your homemade compost to be ready, or if you don't have the room for a compost heap or bin, there is a great range of peat-free, organic composts available, which are more expensive than the alternatives, but I believe it's worth the outlay. For some years now, I have also used a biochar-based compost, which helps establish roots quickly and encourages nutrients and microbial populations in the soil that noticeably improve plant health and productivity.

PEAT-FREE COMPOST If you are not keen on using peat-based composts (and who can blame you, since harvesting peat from lowland bogs affects the wildlife that depends on these habitats as well as adversely effecting local ecosystems and ultimately our environment), there are plenty of alternatives on offer. In the early years of peat-free, it really wasn't a viable alternative as it dried out so quickly, but these days, recipes and ingredients have improved and it's much more effective. Read the label and go for brands that provide plenty of information about how to use and care for the product. Look out for composts that have beneficial additives like biochar, seaweed and mycorrhizal fungi, because these all help container-grown crops.

SOILLESS COMPOST Made from any combination of materials such as peat, coir fibre, bark or vermiculite, these composts are specially created for containers and particular types of plant. They offer good drainage, aeration and a neutral pH. They are also light and, generally speaking, you don't need to apply any feed for the first six weeks.

ERICACEOUS COMPOST This provides the right acidity for crops such as blueberries and cranberries that need soil with a pH level between 4 and 5 (a neutral soil has a pH of 7; alkaline soils have a pH above 7). It is readily available to buy from garden centres, DIY stores or online.

FREE-DRAINING COMPOST Some crops, especially Mediterranean herbs, need a very open, free-draining growing medium. Adding horticultural grit or perlite to general composts helps to provide the right conditions by improving aeration and preventing the compost from becoming waterlogged and compacted. A good ratio to use is 3-parts compost to 1-part horticultural grit.

Compost tips

- Fill containers with compost to about 2.5cm from the top to prevent the soil from washing away over the sides when you water.
- As a rule of thumb, one 20-litre bag of compost will fill a 30cm-diameter pot.
- It is best to use fresh compost each year if you are completely replanting a pot with new plants, but with large containers you could remove only the top two-thirds of compost and replace it with new compost for each planting season. Top-dressing (scraping off the top layer of old compost and refreshing with new compost) each year is sufficient for perennials that are staying in the same container until they need repotting (after three or four years of growth).

Worms ...

The humble earthworm is the unsung hero of the soil. Most of us are probably aware that it's a good thing if you dig a hole in your garden and see lots of worms. However, their contribution to the health and fertility of soil is pretty incredible, and the benefits of having them take up residence in your soil are broader than just the fact that they're churning it up or forming a tasty treat for our feathered friends.

For centuries, worms have been recognised for the vital contribution they make to the overall health and productivity of the soil. Aristotle recognised their importance as the 'intestines of the Earth', and Cleopatra supposedly decreed earthworms as sacred animals, forbidding Egyptian farmers to disturb or remove them from the land for fear it affected the soil's fertility. Of course, Charles Darwin sums up their importance most succinctly:

The plough is one of the most ancient and most valuable of man's inventions; but long before he existed the land was in fact regularly ploughed, and still continues to be thus ploughed by earth-worms. It may be doubted whether there are many other animals which have played so important a part in the history of the world, as have these lowly organised creatures.

From his book *The Formation of Vegetable Mould Through the Action of Worms with Observations on their Habitats*, published in 1883.

The key thing to know is that earthworms chomp their way through all manner of organic matter which, once processed through their guts, transforms into worm casts that are rich with microbial activity, have a high nutrient content and help to improve the soil's structure and improve water retention – all essential benefits for healthy plant growth. To my mind it's a horticultural form of alchemy.

If you don't have soil in your own back yard, don't despair. You can still enjoy the benefits worms bring to the garden by setting up a wormery, as described on page 71. Not only will they create a perfect, friable compost that's ideal for seed sowing or potting up your plants (indoor or outdoor), and produce a liquid that's a fantastic fertiliser, but they'll eat your kitchen waste too – in fact, their appetites are fairly voracious and they will devour kitchen scraps, cooked food scraps, veg peelings, coffee grounds and tea leaves, not to mention hair, wool and vacuum cleaner dust.

... and other wonders

Nitrogen is essential in plant growth, and nitrogen-fixing plants are hugely beneficial in a vegetable garden. While this might sound a little heavy on the horticultural science, it's actually very straightforward. Legumes – such as peas, beans and clover – are also known as nitrogen fixers, which work together with bacteria to collect nitrogen from the atmosphere and store it as they grow (they require very little nitrogen themselves). When the plant dies, it releases the stored nitrogen, which in turn raises the nitrogen levels in the soil, from which other plants will benefit.

It is a great idea to plant nitrogen fixers next to any leafy vegetables (lettuce, silverbeet, cabbage, broccoli, bok choy, etc.), as leafy vegetables are known to require a lot of nitrogen.

Deep-rooted herbs like comfrey, borage and dandelion collect nutrients from deep in the soil and hold this huge variety of nutrients in their leaves. The leaves of these herbs can be chopped off and lightly dug into your soil to act as a fertiliser for nearby plants. Be careful with comfrey in the veg-growing area, as whenever you cut a root a new comfrey plant springs up, so it can become invasive.

Foraged **wild garlic**, winter **salad leaves** and the last
of the **kale**. I was so excited that despite the frost, fresh leaves
have sprouted along the kale stem and at the top, which I'll add to
scrambled eggs or lentil and grain salads. (I like to have a simple tahini
dressing made up in a recycled jam jar, as this really does add a zing
to a lentil salad. Simply combine 1:5 ratio of tahini and yoghurt
with garlic, lemon juice and salt to taste.)

Bees, butterflies and other winged insects

It's Hal's birthday today, and his grandparents have made him the frame of an insect hotel kit so that he can gather the bits and pieces to fill each section. I managed to eke out the required hunter-gathering with a trip to the park and the woods, as well as looking around our garden for pine cones, twigs, leaves, seed heads, snail shells and all the other natural materials that can be used. Bug hotels look really lovely in a garden, and they are an excellent way to help pollinators and natural predators feel at home in your plot. The rewards of showing a little hospitality are well worth the effort, after all, we'd have no food without bees, and would be overrun with unwanted pests without ladybirds, lacewings and other winged insects.

I remember spending many happy hours chasing butterflies when I was a child. We had two buddleias – or butterfly bushes – in our garden, and from June to September they would be alive with a variety of butterfly species, from cabbage to peacock, meadow to tortoiseshell. Forty years on and I'm sad to see that Hal isn't enjoying the same experience. Many butterfly species are steadily declining and it's the same story with bees and many other of our pollinating insects. Whether as a result of disease, which has decimated the bee population; loss of habitats, which are vital for pollinators to make their nest; or the widespread use of pesticides, many of these creatures are struggling to thrive. This is a worry for many reasons, over and above the pleasure of seeing them in our gardens – and the fun of chasing them. Research shows that bees and other insect pollinators are responsible for one in three mouthfuls of our food, and that insect pollinators contribute £440 million to the British economy through their role in fertilising crops.

Thankfully, it's not all bad news. In recent years charities and associations, like the British Beekeepers Association (BBKA), the Butterfly Conservation and the RHS, have drawn attention to this issue through campaigns and initiatives, and it turns out that we growers can make a huge difference to help improve numbers. While actually keeping bees might be unrealistic for most of us, finding a spot for a nest box for solitary bees and bumblebees is easy, not to mention a lifeline to these buzzing insects. You can also grow nectar- and pollen-rich flowers – a container will provide a much-needed source of food and energy for bees, butterflies and other pollinators throughout the year.

You don't need to be a plant expert to know which plants are best for pollinating insects either. The RHS has launched a campaign for garden centres and specialist nurseries to add a sticker to varieties that are 'Perfect for Pollinators'. If you can squeeze a few nectar-rich varieties into beds or in containers, you'll be rewarded with flowers throughout the year and a bountiful supply of fruit and crops, as well as a healthy, happy population of bees and butterflies.

Go for single, simple flowers rather than highly cultivated double-flowered forms, as they often have little or nothing in the way of pollen and nectar. If you're unsure, stick to old-fashioned cottage varieties, as they're easy for insects to feed from.

While pollinators need food during the summer when they're very active, spare a thought from them at other times of the year too. Some species emerge in early spring when there's little sustenance available to them, and now our weather patterns are changing, with milder winters, insects can get confused and come out of hibernation at the wrong time too. Honeybees are active from late winter to autumn, and some other pollinators, including some bumblebees, can be active over winter, so try planting snowdrops, winter-flowering crocus, hellebores and clematis cirrhosa if you have space. Cranesbill, geums and crocus will help in spring, and while there's more choice in summer, borage, marigolds, cosmos, sunflowers, lavender and sweet Williams work well in veg plots, as do those old allotment favourites dahlias and chrysanthemums in the autumn.

There are more than 200 species of wild bees that prefer the quiet life, making individual nest cells for their larvae rather than hanging out in a large colony. This easy-to-make bee hotel will help attract solitary species into your garden.

1. Make (or find) a wooden box and leave it open on one side. It should be 20cm deep but as wide and as high as you like. You can also use clay pipe.

2. Cut bamboo canes into 20cm lengths. You can also use a drill to make holes in small logs. Ensure the 'entrance' to these holes is smooth and splinter free.

3. Fill the box with these canes and logs and place in a sunny spot.

Birthday **rhubarb** – success! Well, I managed a crumble,
but there wasn't enough to make rhubarb cordial.

....

Cardoon leaves – even if they are young and fresh you still need to boil them in water and lemon juice for a few hours to soften, after which you can use them a bit like fennel or artichoke and add to pasta.

....

Wild garlic for a pesto.

April 7th

Sowing outdoors

Depending on your location and, more specifically, your garden's particular microclimate, getting the growing season off to a flying start revolves around a bit of forward planning. Watch the weather and do a little research into when the last frosts will appear. Once you have a rough idea, you then can work backwards to find the optimum seed-sowing window to enable you to start seeds off indoors (see page 62). Generally it's 6–8 weeks, which brings us to March, although you can early-sow as soon as February (assuming your frosts tend to stop wreaking havoc in early May). It's worth clarifying that this is for tender seeds, tomatoes, chillies, basil, courgettes, salads, peas and beans, etc.; the tougher varieties, like beetroot, chard, spinach and carrots, will be able to cope with this later, direct-sowing.

It was wet first thing, but by late morning it has brightened up and is surprisingly warm outside. This is good news because I want to sow some radish and carrots, and when it comes to sowing outdoors, it's all about the soil being the right temperature. You don't need gizmos or to sit bare-cheeked on the soil, as more eccentric growers might suggest (unless you want to give your neighbours a treat/shock). You just need to notice when weeds start to appear – if it's warm enough to get them going, it's time to get sowing (after you've dealt with the weeds, obviously).

I often go for plugs (seedlings that are grown in trays of small cells) because it helps reduce the amount of space I would otherwise need to find for seed trays, and it's a good time-saver too. That said, they are more expensive and mean you don't get to enjoy the pleasure of raising plants from seed.

Radish and carrots are a good choice to direct-sow into the ground as seeds as it's easier to thin them out as seedlings, as opposed to sowing them in seed trays and pricking them out (separating the seedlings into individual plugs or pots). I grow both these crops in big containers, but it's the same method if you're sowing in beds and borders. Prepare the soil so that the top layer is as fine as possible, either by breaking up lumps with a trowel or, for the purists, by using a special soil sieve. I water at this stage, as watering after sowing can disturb the seeds. Radish and carrot seeds are very small, so I take a pinch at a time, scattering on the surface and lightly covering them with compost. If sowing in a container, make sure you leave enough room at the top of the pot or tray to accommodate this top layer when you initially fill it with compost. For larger seeds, such as those of beans and pumpkins, make a hole with a pen or your finger to the appropriate depth, and drop one seed in and cover with compost, repeating at the intervals stated on the seed packet. Sow in a line if you wish, although, as discussed earlier, I often sow in gaps. They should germinate after about two weeks, when you'll see tiny seedlings emerging through the soil. Let them reach about 3cm and have a second pair of 'true' leaves – the first are actually the cotyledons (seed leaf) not actual leaves. Thin them out, by leaving one strong, healthy plant every 10cm – just pull them up by the roots and throw them away.

I've started off sweetcorn, pumpkins, cucumbers and luffas, and it's also time to sow some salad leaves and herbs – lettuce (rocket, oak-leaf lettuce, mizuna) and hardy herbs (coriander, garlic chives, flat-leaf parsley, dill and fennel) can be sown under cover, as well as tomatoes for planting in early May if the weather permits. You can also direct-sow chervil, chives and sage.

Spring onions (grown from plugs planted in February), **lettuce** and a few tiny **radishes**, which I sliced and pickled to liven up and add a bit of crunch to salad wraps.

April 14th

Shade crops

I've never owned a south-facing garden. Some growers will regard this as unfortunate, because the general view is that your gardening wings are clipped if you have to cope with any other aspect. My garden faces south-east, which means I can't sit in the sun with a gin and tonic after 6.30 p.m., even in the height of summer. It's not as bad as it sounds – we have a mixture of sun and shade, and we get to have a drink earlier in the afternoon. Similarly, friends with the dreaded north-facing gardens have learned to adapt, and accept that they have to work with a limited list when it comes to choosing crops that will thrive in their conditions. (They are also expert at soliciting invitations for a summer's-evening drink with friends who have a sunnier aspect.) Then there's the obvious health benefits associated with not having too much sun, and I often find I seek out shade to escape the stifling heat generated in my small urban plot in the height of the summer.

I prefer to look at it this way: While a south-facing garden is, for many, *the dream*, sometimes you can be spoiled for choice, and working with a reduced list of crops that will grow in your plot isn't as bad as you might think. It's the same with growing on a balcony or indoors on a windowsill – while limited space might initially disappoint, the fact is, you can still enjoy some fresh, home-grown ingredients and that's better than nothing.

Growing in the shade

Light levels do affect a plant's ability to grow (sunlight allows them to make the sugar that gives them the energy to grow, and lower sugar

Shade crops

137

production levels leads to a weakened plant, which may die), but there are things you can do if your plot is, on balance, a bit gloomy. If you or your neighbours have any trees whose branches cast shadow, consider thinning them out (check with your neighbours first if they're not in your plot) to allow more light into the garden. Bright colours, or even white, reflect the sunshine, so if you can paint a garden wall or even the raised beds or containers, you will help increase light levels. Adding wheels to

Shade glossary

Full sun: more than six hours of direct sun each day in midsummer.
Light shade: an otherwise sunny site, which is shaded by a high wall or group of trees.
Partial-shade: three to six hours of direct sun each day in midsummer.
Moderate shade: two to three hours of direct sun each day in midsummer.
Heavy shade: less than two hours of direct sun each day in midsummer.

the underside of large, heavy containers enables you to follow the sun, if space allows. Ultimately, if you can ensure your plants have around four hours of sunshine a day, they may be smaller and slower to mature, but you will be rewarded with some crops.

What to grow?

Leafy salads, chard, spinach, cabbage and kale are able to cope with partial shade, as well as beetroot, radish and carrots. Potatoes will put up with less sunshine, and even celery, Brussels sprouts, cauliflower, peas and beans won't sulk too much if they're in some light shade. Herbs like basil, mint, parsley, coriander and oregano will even thank you if they get some respite from the heat each day. Rather than direct-sow seeds destined to grow in some shade, start them off early, in trays or pots, in a bright, sunny spot to encourage a healthy, strong root system. Transplant when seedlings are more robust.

You can even grow your fruit salad in a shaded garden. Raspberries, currants, gooseberries and rhubarb will cope in partial shade, and cooking apples can put up with light shade. And Morello cherry and William's pear trees, as well as redcurrants, white currants and gooseberries, are all ideal types to grow, fan-trained, against east- and north-facing walls.

Peas from early sowing, which actually aren't quite mature, so I pick whole, blanch them – pods and all – and then buzz them up into a perfectly sweet pea puree. A good tip is to plunge them into iced water after boiling, to help them retain that intense colour. Mix with ricotta cheese as a filling for cannelloni, or use as an alternative to pesto over pasta.

Sweetcorn

I first grew sweetcorn on my allotment in London, much to the amusement of the lovely old chap in the plot next door. In those early weeks, my boyfriend at the time and I kept him entertained with our plot preparations. Against our benign neighbour's advice, we had dug every inch of the plot – a full 10 rods (quirkily, allotment plot size is still calculated in 'rods', a measurement that dates back to Anglo-Saxon farming, where one rod was supposedly the length from the back of the plough to the nose of the oxen), the equivalent of 250 square metres, so no mean feat – and undertaken pretty impressive earthworks to level it, edge each bed with sleepers and create a series of weed suppressant-lined mulched paths. To my neighbour's mind this was all wasted effort, and on reflection, while our plot looked pretty and neat, from a productive perspective his rough-and-ready beds and grass paths beat us hands down each season.

On this occasion, I had planted the sweetcorn in two rows, and was told by my neighbour that in doing so, I had 'done it wrong'. He was right, of course, as sweetcorn needs to be planted closely together in a block to increase the chances of being pollinated by the wind. Lesson learned, and since then my sweetcorn plants, grown in the ground and in large containers, have always produced cobs. We picked up a great deal from our neighbour, and our competence (and crops) grew well under his watchful eye (well, critical eye if I'm honest, but time has diminished the effect of his harsh appraisals, and I prefer to look back on the experience through rose-tinted spectacles).

I've also discovered another trick with sweetcorn, and that is to soak the seeds in warm water for an afternoon before potting up. Some types of seed are fussy and require specific techniques to encourage them to

germinate; soaking is one way to encourage larger, wrinkly seeds like peas, beans, corn, pumpkins and squash, while a quick blast in the fridge (stratification) works wonders for apples, sloes, plums and lavender (though you're unlikely to start these off from seed), and creating a nick or rough patch in the seed-coating using a knife or a bit of sandpaper (scarification) can be necessary for beans, prior to soaking.

Varieties

I was intrigued to try 'Snobaby' F1 sweetcorn this year, because it's a great option for small spaces. You can either harvest the corns when small, to use in curries (or to tempt children to eat their veg), or when they're mature they can be dried and used for popping. I did a combination of both of these options: Six container-grown plants (four of which were really strong, two a little weaker) produced a few tasty mini corns, and a couple of cobs that provided popcorn for two film nights. Sow from now until mid June, and plant out in a bed or container in June, ready to be harvested from mid August.

I'd like to try 'Special Swiss', which has a super-sweet flavour and is reported by its producer to be the first new open-pollinated variety to be bred in Europe in modern times. Open-pollination is important as it means it isn't a hybrid, or engineered, variety, which can compromise the flavour and characteristics of the crop (see page 104). There is also a 'Double Red' variety, which will look eye-catching in a small plot, and, of course, 'Glass Gem', which was bred from ancient Cherokee corns and looks amazing with its mix of shiny, colourful kernels that can be ground to make flour or dried for popping.

Harvesting tip

If the silks (the hairlike strands at the top) have turned brown and the ears have entirely filled out, which you can tell by feeling the end of the ear (it should be rounded or blunt rather than pointed), it's time to harvest.

The Three Sisters

In the days of the early settlement of North America, corn was so valuable that it was used as money and traded for other products such as meat and furs. Today it is grown in all continents with the exception of Antarctica. Originally growing in northern, central and southern America, corn was one component of a brilliant triumvirate of crops (along with beans and squash) known as the Three Sisters, which essentially was a way to cultivate the three staple crops in one space. The native northern American tribe, the Iroquois, believed that these were inseparable 'sisters', who needed each other to grow. The sweetcorn is sown on the top of a mound and started off first, followed by beans planted in the middle section, so they can use the corn's height as a support, and squash planted at the base to run along the ground.

Sweetcorn

The advent of modern plant breeding

I was interested to discover that sweetcorn was at the heart of the hybrid breeding programme in the United States. In the early 1900s scientists were developing an open-pollinated breeding programme based on the discoveries of the 'father of genetics', Gregor Mendel, 60 or so years before. Mendel had believed that varieties, if isolated from other varieties, produce seed that, genetically speaking, is the same or very similar to that of its parent (known as 'true to type'). By the 1930s, the modern era of plant breeding had dawned and across the US farmers were able to buy commercially produced hybrid sweetcorn, which had been bred by crossing two different parent varieties, each possessing ideal traits for a new breed, which in the case of sweetcorn was bigger yields and bigger kernels, as well as disease resistance. It's important to note, and relevant to gardeners today, that seed from a hybrid variety can be saved, but will not be true to type. As a point of distinction, the term *heirloom* is used to classify open-pollinated varieties that pre-date this breeding work.

Rocket, more **radishes** and young **mint** leaves.
Delicious used raw, or, of course, save the mint for
the first of the season's mojitos (or mint tea for Hal).

....

Wild garlic for a delicious homemade pesto.

Edible flowers

I've just conducted a straw poll among a small gathering of friends to find out their thoughts about edible flowers. It transpires that they are the horticultural equivalent of marmite, polarising opinion between those who feel they're unnecessary decoration and those who think they add texture, flavour and colour to a dish.

I must confess that for years I agreed with the former opinion but the truth was I hadn't really tried them. I was quite surprised when I tasted my first nasturtium flowers several years back when I was visiting a friend. As we chatted and walked around the productive beds, he offered me freshly picked fruit and veg to try. Among the titbits was a beautifully bold orange nasturtium. I was completely bowled over by its peppery flavour. Later that year I began researching my first book, which involved visiting kitchen gardens all over the country. It turned out that the chefs wanted to eat all, or as much of a crop as possible if they were going to invest time growing it – an equivalent to the nose-to-tail approach advocated by butchers. Combining an adventurous spirit and thrifty values, the chefs revelled in the harvest of bolted rocket flowers as well as the more traditional violas, not to mention untold numbers of courgette flowers (I discovered Le Manoir uses a staggering 200 flowers a day during the summer). But rather than use them to decorate ice cubes, these flowers are an integral part of the final dish created by the chefs, adding an intense flavour or a splash of colour to highlight the main ingredient. Mark Cox, gardener for the Ethicurean restaurant in Bristol, was very partial to an electric daisy bud – little yellow button flowers that leave your tongue tingling as if you have licked a 9-volt battery (I recommend trying them – the flowers, that is, not the batteries), and grows a significant amount of 'Rat's Tail' radish for the award-winning chefs, brothers Iain and Matthew Pennington, which is cultivated for its crisp, crunchy seed pods rather than its roots. Meanwhile Simon Rogan from L'Enclume in The Lakes uses chrysanthemum shoots and mallow flowers (try mallow 'Zebrina' as an easy-to-grow cottage-garden type perennial for its slightly nutty flavour), among many others, to create his Michelin-starred dishes.

There are a surprising number of edible herbaceous flowers, which you might have otherwise thought were just pretty ornamentals that play no role in a veg plot. Growing some or all of these plants will give you the opportunity to create your own potager, or mix of flowers and edibles. Obviously, if you're unsure which flowers are safe to eat, check online before picking.

For sunny borders or containers, combine daylilies, hollyhocks and sweet Williams. Daylilies, which need a good free-draining soil (so add plenty of grit if you're growing in a container) can be treated much in the same way as courgette flowers: stuffed and sautéed, or chopped and added to stir-fries, while hollyhock petals can be used to make a delicately flavoured syrup, added to salads, or crystallised to decorate cakes. Keep these fast-growing plants well watered and cut back to 15cm from the ground in the autumn. The purple-blue spires of Mexican giant hyssop (Agastache 'Blue Fortune') are a great contrast to the billowy blooms above, and their minty flowers have a touch of aniseed flavouring, perfect for a tea and to flavour oil, vinegar and butter, as well as used in pasta or other savoury dishes. Reaching 1m in height, these are best for the middle or back of a border. For late-summer flavour, add pineapple sage to this triumvirate and use it in Vietnamese and Thai recipes. Tuberous begonias flower from July to October, and cope in full sun or semi-shade. Their colourful petals provide a crispy texture and lemon flavour, and can be used as a dip for yoghurts and served as a starter, or sliced in sandwiches or on salads.

Try autumn crocus (a poor man's saffron), calendula, cornflowers, rose petals and violets to add natural colouring to icing, frosting and sugar, while crystallised scented pelargoniums and dianthus make beautiful cake decorations.

Edible flower tips

- Pick young flowers and buds on dry mornings, before the sun becomes too strong, when the colour and flavours are at their most intense.
- For best results use flowers immediately, or refrigerate in a plastic bag for a couple of days.
- Generally, only the petals are used, so discard stamens, pistil and calyx of large flowers like hollyhocks, roses, lilies and hibiscus. The bitter 'heel' at the base of the petal should always be removed.

Tomatoes

I don't get terribly excited by my birthday these days, however I was tickled pink that my order of tomato seedlings arrived today – definitely my kind of birthday present, especially as I was able to head straight out into the greenhouse to pot them up.

Tomatoes are the most popular home-grown crop for first-time and experienced gardeners alike, and it's not surprising because they are easy to start from seed and, depending on the variety, produce an abundant crop of tasty fruits. While there are plenty of sweet, juicy varieties to choose from, many of which are bred to cope with our climate (in other words, where endless sunny days to ripen the fruits aren't guaranteed), it is

worth giving careful consideration to the type of tomato you're going to grow, bearing in mind your particular growing conditions. Whichever variety you choose, sunlight is important and the more they have, the more delicious their flavour. It's not *impossible* to achieve the sensational flavour of tomatoes grown (and eaten) in the Mediterranean, but for most varieties a long, hot summer will make all the difference, and becomes essential if you're growing any of the larger-sized types. However, if temperatures soar upwards of

29°C, provide a little shade once the flowers appear, as they can suffer in the extreme heat and fall off.

Available space will also influence the variety you choose. Tomatoes are divided into two groups: tall (cordon or indeterminate, if you want to get technical) or dwarf (bush or determinate). Tall plants require a bit of attention by way of removing unwanted side shoots, and tying stems to a cane support as they grow. Reaching more than 60cm in height, they are best grown in the ground (in a greenhouse or in a sheltered, sunny border), in grow bags or in large containers. Pinch out the tip of the main stem when they've reached the top of the support to help concentrate the remainder of

the plant's growth into the five or six trusses (shoots coming from the main stem) that should already have appeared on the plant (remove any more than that, so the plant doesn't get too stressed). Fruits ripen on the trusses on an ongoing basis throughout the summer, and if you're lucky, until the first frosts.

Dwarf tomato plants need no attention other than feeding and watering, and are also perfect for hanging baskets, which has the added benefit of filling an often-empty vertical space in a small plot. They are also great if you want to try another crop in their space, as once their blossom starts setting they stop growing and their energy goes into producing their fruit all at once – great news if you're off on holiday at the end of the summer or like to batch-cook tomato sauce. Obviously this means you won't have tomatoes for an extended period, although growing several different varieties will extend the harvesting timeframe, if you have enough room.

While I tend to go for plugs, seeds can be started indoors as early as February (see page 62), and if you choose an early variety, this means you could be harvesting in June. Otherwise, anytime between March and April is a good time for sowing tomatoes. Sow a few seeds in a small pot and cover with compost, and when the seedlings are big enough to handle, transplant each seedling into a 7.5cm pot. This year I'm going to try potting them on a second time, to help improve the root mass and allow the little nodules that appear a little way up the stem to have contact with soil to further help them develop into sturdy, healthy plants. If you're planting out in the ground, add plenty of organic matter and leave about 45cm between them and other plants as they have a deep root system, and stick to just two plants in a grow bag. Mulch after planting so that you help retain moisture and provide additional nutrition, remembering not to push the mulch up to the plant's stem. After this, remember to feed them; all tomatoes will benefit from a high-potash feed every week – another one to go on the Feed Friday list.

Over the years I've repeatedly made the mistake of letting the plants dry out and then giving them a long drink to try and rectify the situation. In actual fact, this creates more issues than it solves, causing either the unsightly black blotches of blossom end rot or the fruit to split. It also impairs the flavour and texture. It's really worth watering little and often (daily for containers in hot weather) to ensure your crop is as juicy and sweet as possible. Other problems to watch out for are discoloured leaves (usually older ones), which can indicate a lack of magnesium and can be remedied with a magnesium feed, as well as removing the now-unnecessary leaves, and streaks or a distorted surface on a leaf, which can be the Mosaic virus, in which case it's sadly best to cut your losses and discard the plant before it infects others. If this does occur, remember to wash any tools or pots that came into contact with the diseased plant.

If you can, it's worth growing a variety of tomatoes to provide an interesting collection as well as hedging your bets against the weather...

Cherry tomatoes top the list of the most common variety to grow (I'm willing to bet many of us grew them in a nursery class at school), and for good reason – their small fruits suit our climate and they produce vines laden with them, even on a sunny balcony. 'Gardener's Delight' (a heritage variety), 'Moneymaker' and 'Sungold' are widely available,

reliable, even in cooler weather, and are deliciously sweet. I would also encourage looking at other heritage varieties, which aren't bred to be so incredibly sweet, and have more interesting flavours that add something new to salads and sauces. 'Lemon Tree' is a sunny, lemon-drop-shaped variety that is really worth a try, as is 'Black Cherry', which is just sweet enough and looks amazing too.

'Red Pear' is a lovely sweet-tasting, small plum tomato, though 'Giulietta' is suited to cooler climates and produces a larger fruit. 'Tigerella' has a sharp flavour that works well in salads, and is a favourite of mine because it has the most beautiful skin, firm flesh and a good flavour.

This year, I'm going to try the beefsteak 'Costoluto Fiorentino', which has done well in recent trials. Last year I grew 'Big Brandy', but found it a bit disappointing – though I think my container was just too small to really give it enough water and nutrients. I also want to try the incredibly strange heirloom variety called 'Banana Legs', which is described as being great in salads, with thick, meaty flesh that is also ideal for making into sauces ... what more could you want!

Tomato tips

- Water little and often and use a high-potash feed each week.
- Ensure plants have as much sunlight as possible.

Spring onions and **little gem lettuce** – lightly sauté in a splash of olive oil, then transfer to a casserole dish with a slug of wine, a bit of stock, and season. Cook gently for about half an hour and just before serving, add a few handfuls of peas. Enjoy as a side dish. An ideal recipe if the lettuce is a little bitter, as its flavour sweetens as it cooks. Sauté leek with it too, if it's in season.

Luffas

Whenever I think of my granny, I remember she always took great care with her appearance. Her dressing table was filled with bottles and creams, but it was the luffas (also spelled loofahs) that were always on the side of her avocado-coloured bath, that stick in my mind the most. It may not sound so funny now, we even use luffas as sustainable kitchen scourers, but in the late 1970s this was impressively avant-garde. They always looked so exotic compared to the limp flannel that hung over our tap at home. While my baths were the briefest affairs – a quick dunk – I imagine my granny luxuriated in a bubble-filled tub. In fact, I'm willing to bet she wore a towelling turban as she soaked, too. (Well, if you used a luffa, you would, wouldn't you.)

I have since discovered that luffas are members of the gourd family – I wish I had known that while my granny was still alive (I was convinced they were sea sponges, harvested from the ocean); she would have been delighted to have had a steady supply from her own garden.

My granny was ahead of her time in terms of sustainability, as a natural luffa is far better than having cloth flannels that need washing, or synthetic sponges that ultimately end up in landfill. They are easy to grow, and a food source, too, so it's well worth finding a spot for them in a greenhouse or on a windowsill if you can – if for no other reason than to grow a year's worth of Christmas presents for your family.

Sow in late March and plant out from late April to May. Pick young fruits in August and treat like courgettes, or leave to mature into a luffa, which can be harvested from October onwards. The longer you wait, the drier the outer skin becomes (it eventually turns brown and brittle, like heavy paper), although you can harvest them when they're still green, but the fibrous inside will need to be left to dry for longer. Remove the outer skin, and then extract the seeds by knocking the luffa against a hard surface and spread them out to dry, ready to sow the following season. Wash the luffa to remove excess fibres, leave it to dry, and in a few days it will be ready to use.

Wet garlic and **rocket**. I'm always tempted to eat all my garlic at this point, but worry I'm being greedy, so leave some in the ground to mature. The few that I do pull deserve to be celebrated and cooked with the appropriate reverence. I get a fruit and veg box from a delivery service, and they suggest you add chopped wet garlic to tortillas and a medley of seasonal green veg, which are tasty dishes, but to my mind, you can't beat slowly roasting them to savour the mild, sweet flavour.

Cucumbers

For some inexplicable reason, I hadn't grown cucumbers until last year. I like them (a cucumber sandwich with salt is really hard to beat), and Hal eats a chunky slice in his packed lunch every now and then, but somewhere in the back of my mind I thought they were difficult to grow. I'm not sure where I'd got that idea from, but funnily enough, a friend said the same thing to me this morning. She had asked what I'd been up to, to which I gave the rather un-rock-'n-roll reply: 'planting cucumber plugs'.

'I didn't think you could grow them in our climate', she remarked, making more of a statement than the beginnings of a conversation – not all my friends are green-fingered. Happily, I can debunk our unfounded scepticism – there are lots of cucumber varieties that can be grown under glass as well as in our rather wet and cold climate. And more than that, they're incredibly prolific when they get going. I also loved the fact that I had a steady supply of gherkins if I picked them as babies (my understanding is that a gherkin *is* a baby cucumber – it comes from the Dutch word gurken, which means small pickled cucumber). But I was growing a standard cucumber variety, 'Marketmore', so this year I'm going to try 'Cornichon de Paris', which is a French heirloom variety that is actually used as a gherkin. Given that some shop-bought cucumbers can be two weeks old by the time they reach the shelves, I think it's definitely worth squeezing them into the veg plot or greenhouse if you can, so you can taste the difference of a freshly picked home-grown cucumber. Cucumber 'La Diva' is a great mini cucumber that can be grown indoors or outside, as can the larger 'Romanesco' and the brightly coloured yellow 'Soleil'.

Whether you choose an indoor or outdoor variety, cucumbers need plenty of sun and warmth (though I'm not suggesting you go to the lengths that the Roman emperor, Tiberius, did by demanding his slaves wheeled cucumbers around in carts so that they could catch the sun and grow better). They also need regular watering, otherwise they can taste bitter. Sow seeds between February and June, and if trans-planting outdoors, harden off after the risk of frosts has passed, before planting out in June when temperatures should be warm enough for them. They'll need supporting, so use a cane and tie new growth in. Feed once the flowers appear, and if the variety you've chosen bears male and female flowers, remove the male ones as they can make the fruits taste bitter. (The female flowers are easy to spot as they have an immature fruit behind them.)

Cucumber mosaic virus can be an issue because there is no treatment – plants should be thrown away if they show any signs (a yellow mosaic pattern). Powdery mildew is another disease that affects cucumber plants – picking infected leaves off will help here – and keep an eye out for aphids, removing and squashing them by hand if they appear. While you might have to do battle with a critter or two, or pick off the odd

leaf, don't let this put you off from growing them because you're likely to get a decent harvest, which will be a welcome addition to summer salads.

It's also a good time to sow kale seeds, although you can choose any time during the spring as it is perfectly willing to germinate when it's cold or warm. We are great fans of kale (well, I am), so I find space for it dotted throughout the borders, whether it's in full sun or a bit of shade. I wouldn't direct sow, although you can, because

birds (especially the pair of pigeons that eat our June berries) love it too, so I would be looking to transplant seedlings when they've developed a good set of leaves and look robust enough to cope with a nibble here and there. Or, do as I do, and buy plugs ready to plant in May or June and again at the end of the summer for winter supplies. If you have room, you can successively sow/plant kale from February to August.

Elderflowers

This year, elderflower became a byword for 'just one more trip to our local woods'. When I was young, we were lucky enough to have an enormous elderflower in our garden, but apart from picking the dark purple berries to put in water to make 'a potion', I don't recall ever making cordial or wine. I haven't got round to doing it as an adult either – work is usually at its busiest at this time of year, especially if I'm working on the Chelsea Flower Show television coverage, and before I know it the flowers are fading, their pollen spent, and I've missed it again.

This spring, I was determined to address this omission from my culinary endeavours with foraged food. The universe, however, appeared to have different plans and the whole process of making elderflower cordial turned out to be a lengthy fiasco. Dear reader, this cautionary tale reminds us it is ALWAYS worth reading the method first, and focusing on the job in hand, rather than trying to do several things at once and rushing. More speed, less haste, as my parents infuriatingly used to tell me.

I only have a small variegated pot-grown elderflower in my garden, 'Variegata', which I grew for my last book, *Grow Your Own Botanicals*. Though dwarf varieties like mine are available, and elderflowers are a lovely specimen, this isn't a sensible shrub to grow if space is an issue – you won't have to travel far to find them growing wild instead. Easy to spot – look for the white sprays of flowers – they tend to look pretty unkempt and are usually found in hedgerows, footpaths or at the edge of woods.

This year my elderflower has produced a single bloom, so as the recipe calls for 30 heads, I needed to forage the other 29.

The first trip to our local wood, where elderflowers are dotted among hedges and riverbanks, was a complete success – a sunny morning

(elderflowers are best picked after the sun has had a chance to open the buds, but before insects have gathered the scented pollen), an enjoyable stroll and plenty of fun to be had gathering the abundant flowers. I even managed to keep them upright so as not to lose any pollen, which gives the drink its flavour.

Uncharacteristically, I prepared the flowers the moment we returned home (I'm prone to leaving things by the sink 'to do later', and end up making whatever I'm making in a panic because they're clearly 'on the turn' and *must* be dealt with immediately). By late morning our spoils were steeping in my biggest heavy pan, filled with freshly boiled water.

Elderflower cordial

- 1kg granulated sugar
- 1.5 litres boiling water
- 50g citric acid, or juice of 2 lemons if the cordial doesn't need to be stored
- Zest of 3 large lemons
- 30 elderflower heads, stalks removed

Method

Dissolve the sugar in a pan of boiling water. Add the citric acid or lemon juice, and the lemon zest. (Citric acid prevents the cordial from fermenting, so if you're not keeping yours for too long, there's no need to use it.)

Gently wash (shake) the elderflowers to remove any insects and add the flowers to the sugar syrup. Cover and leave to stand for 1–2 days, stirring morning and night.

Strain the elderflower cordial through muslin and decant into sterilised bottles. Keep in a cool, dark place for up to 2 months. Once opened, refrigerate and use within a month.

All was well until later that evening, when I was re-reading the recipe and realised that rather than briefly immersing them in cold water to remove insects and dirt, I had vigorously swished them and left them to soak for half an hour while I got on with another pressing job. A quick sniff of the elderflower-infused liquid suggested I had managed to remove most of the pollen (and therefore flavour) because it had hardly any scent.

The following day, we returned to the woods to collect a second stash. This time, I carefully removed the motley crew of little black bugs, fine spiders and discoloured petals by hand before steeping them. I had been so fixated on preserving as much pollen as I could, that I'd completely omitted to remove the stems and stalks. By the time I realised, the liquid had already turned green (think Bridget Jones' blue-twine-dyed soup). With slightly less enthusiasm, Hal and I set off the following morning to harvest a third batch of flowers, which was a little more laborious as our last two visits had significantly depleted the flowers, and many of the largest ones were now too high for me to reach and required Hal to sit on my shoulders. This time, I patiently carried out all the prep work, learning from my previous mistakes. After covering the flowers with my homemade sugar syrup and lemon zest, I sprinkled in the citric acid ... only realising too late, as it fizzed madly, that I'd used bicarb of soda rather than citric acid. (Beautifully styled shelves filled with jars of decanted ingredients might look nice, but they can also trip up all but the most eagle-eyed cook.)

Needless to say, tempers were a little fraught at the suggestion of a fourth elderflower-gathering expedition, and matters weren't improved by the scarcity of the flowers.

However, our perseverance paid off and today we are rewarded with three bottles of utterly delicious cordial, which we labelled 'If at first you don't succeed ... elderflower cordial'.

Elderflowers also make delicious sparkling wine, hollandaise, fritters and jam, and can be mixed into cakes and infused in jellies and ice cream. Their delicate floral flavour goes really well with rhubarb and gooseberries, too, as it balances out their tartness.

A note about foraging

As with gathering any of nature's spoils, avoid busy roadsides if possible, as fumes and dirt can be an issue, as is harvesting at ground level, where animals are likely to have taken a pee.

Spinach, spring onions, new potatoes from Mum and, of course, **elderflowers**. I'll use spinach raw or cooked in most things, and I'm even managing to get Hal not to turn his nose up. Spring onions and new potatoes screams potato salad. I realise to some it's sacrilegious to smother the tasty golden nuggets in mayonnaise, but in our household it's Mum's potato salad all the way. Don't forget to add hard-boiled eggs (you want to catch them just before the yolk turns pale and powdery, so around seven minutes from cold).

Pumpkins

If you have kids, growing their own pumpkin for Halloween is guaranteed to get them excited. Actually, I still find it great fun, so scrap that – this is one for kids of *all* ages.

While they are really easy to grow, with lovely large seeds that germinate quickly and produce a plant that puts on lots of lush foliage and, before too long, brightly coloured fruits, the main thing about a home-grown jack-o'-lantern is that it will give you the edge when it comes to creating a spooky display on 31 October.

Over the years, I've commissioned a number of magazine articles showing the most imaginative pumpkin-carving methods – the first time I saw a contributor artfully position the stringy insides to look as though the pumpkin was vomiting, I was pretty impressed (it certainly beat my uninspiring efforts of triangular-shaped eyes and mouth), and I never tired of the magical effect created by drilling randomly sized holes all over the pumpkin. But to my mind, a pumpkin covered with customised warty, gnarly scars (created by scratching a design into the skin of a young pumpkin, which develops into the most gruesome-looking scars as it grows) wins hands down.

I mistakenly thought a jack-o'-lantern was another name for a large orange pumpkin – the bigger the better. But it turns out that they could be carved from any root vegetable (pumpkins, turnips and swedes were first used to ward off spirits during Halloween in the nineteenth century in Ireland, the Scottish Highlands and Somerset). This removes any guilt I might have otherwise felt for making Hal use a variety of smaller pumpkins and squashes to carve his scary faces, which not only look more interesting on the doorstep, but also are far more delicious when it comes to using up the discarded flesh in soups, or roasting them and using in salads. The fact is, traditional Halloween pumpkins are all well and good for making a sickly sweet pie, but they simply don't compare to the variety of delicate, nutty, earthy-flavoured pumpkins, squashes and gourds on offer to the home grower.

Another reason to try a smaller variety is space-related: You will need a large sized patch if you're hoping to grow a huge pumpkin, though in theory you could train the leaves off the ground to free up space, but then there's the issue of the big, heavy fruit that will need supporting. You can try curling the stems around the plant if you're really keen for a big 'un, being careful not to snap them as you do it. Pumpkins are also hungry beasts, sometimes grown on compost heaps to satisfy their appetite, so it stands to reason that if you want a champion pumpkin, it will need plenty of room to spread and enough soil from which to draw the required nutrients. Smaller varieties and squashes on the other hand can be successfully grown in pots or tucked into the corner of a bed and trained up a teepee or up-and-over an arbour. Last year Hal grew the ghostly grey squash 'Crown Prince' in a bucket balanced on the wall, along which the vines could enjoy a free run as they basked in the sun. He had to keep an eye on the moisture of the soil and feed it regularly, but it seemed happy enough and he was pleased with his efforts, despite the midsummer drama when his kitten tipped the bucket off the wall, which severed one of the vines and left him with only one squash. We're going to try this variety again this year, along with a mini pumpkin called 'Munchkin' (which is another tasty type with small seeds that can be eaten whole), and take the necessary steps to protect them from his inquisitive feline friend.

Pumpkins and squashes are part of the cucurbit family, which also includes gourds, courgettes, marrows and cucumbers, and in my experience they're super easy to grow from seed. They can be started off in pots indoors, but as it's a busy seed-sowing time of year and space is always an issue for me, I leave it until now to directly sow, either in beds or containers. The first pair of leaves the seedlings produce (cotyledons) are big and lush, so susceptible to slugs and snails – be vigilant! If you have problems with these pests, and if it's been a particularly damp spring or your part of the world is still fairly cold, then get them going indoors, planting them out when they're more sizeable and robust. Don't forget to harden them off prior to planting, which just means pop them outside for an hour or two in the afternoons the week before you plan to plant them somewhere sheltered and in the sun.

I cover mine with upturned plastic bottles sometimes, which is a good barrier to pests, though not 100 per cent foolproof, as slugs and snails can emerge from the soil within these makeshift cloches – impressive but annoying! Pumpkins and squashes are incredibly thirsty, so make sure they don't dry out if it's a warm, dry summer and once they produce flowers, decide on whether you'd prefer one large pumpkin or several smaller ones, removing the unwanted blooms if the former is the

case. Once the fruits start to develop, put something under them so they don't rot (straw, a tile or an upturned seed tray), and feed every fortnight with a high potash liquid feed, until it's time to pick them for Halloween. Of course, if you're not using them on Halloween, harvest them when they sound hollow if tapped and definitely before the first frosts.

Strawberries and **spinach**. While eating fresh strawberries is hard to beat, I've found the best way to cope with the odd few here and there over the seasons is to use them in smoothies. I pop in a few spinach leaves when Hal isn't looking and bingo, two of his five-a-day, sorted. (Thank heaven for single-serve blenders that blitz the leaves so completely, they are invisible to even the most eagle-eyed 11-year-old.)

Companion planting

I was lucky enough to work with the incredibly talented Carol Klein when I was a researcher for *BBC Gardeners' World Magazine*. On one occasion, she came to stay the night before a shoot, and while it was lovely to see her, I was excruciatingly nervous about her seeing my garden. I was writing *Grow Your Own Botanicals* at the time and my tiny plot was stuffed to the gunnels with around 80 different varieties of herbs – I'm not sure I'd have won any design awards for the over-flowing borders and countless pots. Thankfully she arrived late in the evening when it was too dark to see outside, but I couldn't put off the inevitable in the morning. 'You love green', she said tactfully. While I inwardly cringed about my debatable flair for garden design, it also got me thinking that though I do actually love green, creating a garden that lacks colour is an easy trap to fall into when growing herbs and, for that matter, vegetables. The garden did have billowing clouds of purple catmint, splashes of vivid indigo salvias and mauve verbena, elegant white foxglove spires and zinging pops of orange calendula, but by and large, the beds were a tapestry of green. The same can be said for a vege-table garden, where green leafy foliage dominates. There's no reason why you can't have both colour *and* edible crops, in fact there's plenty of choice when it comes to colourful crops: red cabbage, rainbow chard, purple podded peas and beans and, I've seen in the latest seed catalogue, a new bright pinky-mauve kale. However, I'm drawn to the old-fashioned idea of a potager, where edible and ornamental plants combine to create a picture-perfect plot, filled with produce and blooms to delight both palette and eye. When space is an issue, growing orna-mentals could be considered a luxury, but I would argue that, carefully chosen, they bring plenty of perks to the party. For a start, the more flowers, the more enticing your plot for pollinating insects, and that means high rates of crop fertilisation, which ultimately means bigger harvests. While ornamentals play a supporting role when crops are at the height of production, they take the lead at the beginning and end of the growing season, when the veg patch is looking a little bare as seedlings are establishing themselves, or in the last throes of summer, when many crops are starting to fade.

In *An Ear to the Ground*, Ken Thompson suggests that growing different types of plants benefits the garden because, as is so often the case in life, the whole is greater than the sum of the parts, which is particularly significant when trying to battle unwanted pests. In other words, it's time to deploy the idea of companion planting.

According to Ken, a study conducted by University of Warwick researchers revealed that scent plays a huge role in pests preying upon a crop. They land on anywhere that's green and use their feet to 'taste' the plant. If it's delicious, they fly to a few other plants nearby, and if then it tastes the same, they're confident to lay their eggs. If they land on a plant they don't enjoy, a marigold next to a tomato, for example, they'll try a few more times, but if they're left unsure about the type of plant, they'll move on. Ken's point is that rows of vegetables provide the optimum conditions for pests and ensure their 'test flights' always produce positive results. Mixing it up (a great principle for life in general, don't you think?) will keep them, quite literally, on their toes. He also pushes the boundaries further by suggesting that any alternative 'green crop' will work – it doesn't have to be the traditional pairings. Clover or weeds will work just as well as curry plants, marigolds or onions, according to Ken's wisdom. There is a caveat to this, and that is timing. You have to ensure the decoy plant doesn't overwhelm your crop – so try to match vigour for vigour with your choice of plant, which can be another crop, and don't be tempted to squeeze them too closely in. There's also the more whimsical notion of plants helping one another – Bill Withers' song 'Lean On Me' springs to mind. For example, lettuce and celery struggle if they receive too much summer afternoon sun.

In contrast, aubergine and chilli plants love full sunlight. So by planting lettuce among or to the south-east of the aubergine and chilli, both will be receiving their preferred amount of sun, and will grow better. With so much bonhomie in the air, here's a quick list of my favourite best-buddy planting combos:

Borage, when planted nearby, helps **squash** with pollination and improves the flavour of tomatoes and strawberries.	**Nasturtiums** keep whitefly away from **radish** and **brassicas** – a sacrificial crop, remove infested nasturtium plants throughout the season. Nasturtiums also help improve the flavour of the veg.	**Mint** repels slugs from **lettuce.** Lettuce grows well with **beans, beets, carrots, cucumbers, onions, strawberries** and **radish.**
Basil keeps insects away from **tomatoes,** as well as enhancing their flavour.	**Beans** and **peas,** the great nitrogen fixers, boost the growth of **brassicas, carrots, cucumbers, sweetcorn, lettuce, aubergines, radish** and **strawberries.**	**Onions** and other **alliums** such as chives, garlic, leeks and shallots protect a wide range of plants, including **roses.**
Tomato growth can be enhanced if they are grown with **onions, basil, parsley, marigolds** and **nasturtiums.**	**Cucumbers** grow well with **beans, peas, corn, lettuce, onions, marigolds, sunflowers** and **nasturtiums.**	**Sunflowers** improve the growth and productivity of **cucumbers** if grown together in a border.
Carrots grow well next to **lettuce, onions** and **peas.**	**Peppers,** both hot and sweet, like to be grown with **basil** and **onions.**	**Garlic** improves the flavour of **beetroot.**

Incompatible planting

Like people, some plants just don't get along, and it's really not worth forcing the issue. For that reason:

Keep **strawberries** away from **brassicas**.	**Beans** or **peas** won't appreciate being stuck together with **onions, garlic** or **chives** as they stunt their growth.	**Garlic** stunts the growth of **sage, parsley, asparagus** and **strawberries**.
Basil hinders **sage**.	**Carrots** don't like **tomatoes, potatoes, brassicas** or **dill**.	**Lettuce** won't do well next to **brassicas** or **parsley**.

Young **geranium** leaves, **mint** and **thyme**. I finely chop and add geranium leaves to butter and serve on freshly baked scones, as well as using them to make scented sugar. This is super easy – simply bruise a few leaves and add to a jar of sugar, between two or three layers. Leave somewhere warm for up to four weeks, allowing the sugar to take on the subtle flavour. I grow rose-scented geraniums, but other varieties offer different scents, from spicy orange 'Charity' to ginger 'Torrento', and from lemon-rose 'Mabel Grey' to sherbet 'Lady Scarborough'.

....

A bit of a herb-fest: **fennel** (either buy seeds to sow in spring or young plants, which can be planted from the spring to the autumn), **thyme** and **rosemary** to flavour the dough to make crackers, which sounds super impressive but in reality is incredibly easy and transforms picnics into a gourmet feast if you're eating cheese with homemade biscuits.

Herb crackers

- 350g plain flour
- 1 tsp salt
- 60ml olive oil
- Handful of herbs

Method

Preheat the oven to 200°C. Mix the flour, salt, olive oil and approximately 200ml water to make the dough. Add in a few handfuls of finely chopped herbs of your choice (add as little or as much as you'd like – it's really down to taste).

Work the dough and then cut in half, rolling out until it's about 2mm thick. Lay on a parchment paper-lined baking tray and prick with a fork to stop it from rising. Sprinkle seeds and nuts on top too, if you like – we like to sprinkle on some sea salt, too.

Cook for about 10 minutes. When the dough is lightly golden, take out of the oven and cut into rectangles. Store in a container with a lid.

Summer

Continue sowing lettuce, herbs, beetroot, chard, spinach and spring onions in trays or pots, and direct-sow beans, peas and spring cabbage.

Plant out seedlings and plugs of salads, radish, Brussels sprouts, cabbage, kale, celeriac, peppers (sow as tomato and chilli), tomatoes, sweetcorn and leeks.

Pinch out side-shoots, stake and tie in tomatoes and cucumbers.

Keep on top of weeds.

Earth-up potatoes.

Set up a watering and feeding schedule (e.g. Feed Friday).

Cut back summer-fruiting raspberry canes once they have finished fruiting.

Chit and plant out new potatoes for harvesting in time for Christmas.

Quinoa

My quinoa seeds arrived today and I have to confess, when I opened the packet it occurred to me I'd been rather stupid in ordering them online at £3.75 per 10g when I have a 150g pack in my cupboard, which cost me £1.99. I was further embarrassed when a friend popped around for a cup of tea, saw the small packet, and had hysterics that I was now buying my quinoa in impossibly small amounts. Had I found a new source of incredibly precious grains, she wondered? No. I had in fact bought quinoa to grow. She looked at me quizzically. Nothing more needed to be said.

What was I thinking?

Common sense tells me that, as long as they are organic and aren't pre-soaked nor toasted, the seeds from the 150g pack can be successfully germinated. It's basic horticulture that plants produce seeds that, well, grow the following season into a plant.

In theory this is the case, but I'm relieved to discover that purchasing raw seeds 'to sow' rather than using my 'edible' seeds was actually not as silly as it sounds.

It turns out that raw quinoa seeds actually come coated in a compound, saponin, that naturally repels pests and also contains the necessary nutrition for the seed to grow. Saponin tastes bitter, so it's removed by commercial machinery from the quinoa that is sold to eat. You can rinse raw quinoa but there's a chance the saponin won't be completely removed. Plus there's the issue of losing the fine grains through a sieve.

However, this actually depends on where you buy your quinoa from. The varieties grown in the UK and sold in supermarkets don't actually have the saponin coating, so there's no need to 'process' it.

I'm a little bit late, as you can start seeds off in April, sowing directly in prepared ground, or in a large container that gets plenty of sun. This is one time it might be worth being traditional and sowing in a row, or a deliberate shape or pattern, as the seedlings may be mistaken for a weed as they begin to germinate. Eventually reaching about 2m in height, it's probably best sown at the back of a border or against a wall where it won't cast too much shade, unless, of course, that's helpful. Sow a few seeds every few centimetres; you want to end up with one healthy plant with about 25cm of space around it – I'm aiming for 10 plants, which should give me about 450g of grain (a supermarket-packet's worth). After sowing, make sure the ground is moist but not soggy. Once the plants are established, mulch around them to help retain moisture and prevent weeds (see page 32 for mulching advice).

Water regularly and harvest when the plant starts to turn brown in the autumn, allowing the seeds to dry before removing from the stalk (run your hands up the stalk to 'strip' the grains off), blow away any dirt or debris and lay the grains out somewhere to dry, ready to be stored in an airtight container. Remove the bitter saponin coating by soaking and then rinsing the grains several times before cooking. The young, tender leaves can be used in salads throughout the growing season.

QUINOA 101

WHILE GENERALLY thought of as a grain, horticulturally speaking, quinoa is a relative of spinach, beets and chard, and we eat the seed as opposed to the grain (making it an edible fruit).

It is packed with essential amino acids and minerals, a great source of protein and high in fibre. In the main it is gluten-free, too (though there are other varieties that aren't, so check the packaging).

Use as an alternative to rice, couscous and even for porridge or in baking (see opposite).

Quinoa apple cake

- 170g quinoa
- 125g self-raising flour
- 2 apples, cut into chunks
- 125g soft brown sugar
- 100g melted butter

- 125g raisins
- 1 tsp ground cinnamon
- 1 tsp ground ginger
- Pinch of freshly grated nutmeg
- Pinch of salt

Method

Preheat the oven to 175°C. Boil the quinoa in water for 10 minutes until tender. Drain thoroughly and then mix in the rest of the ingredients. Pour the mixture into a greased loaf tin and cook for about 50 minutes until brown. Enjoy fresh from the oven, or cold.

Juneberries and **strawberries**. Depending on the amount you harvest, juneberries make a tasty jam. For smaller bounties, steep a few handfuls in a bottle of gin or vodka. Leave for a few months and add homemade sugar syrup to taste. This year we have a bumper crop and I did manage to pick enough to make jam and gin, before a pair of pigeons had the chance to demolish them all.

....

Beetroot. I roast beetroot with garlic and cumin until soft and caramelised, and then buzz up with yoghurt to make a vibrantly pink and delectable dip. Alternatively, sneak a bit of beetroot in with a smoothie.

Quinoa

How to tackle aphids

The garden is bathed in sunlight this afternoon. Everything looks lush, green, happy and healthy. The fennel is frothing, its feathery bronzed foliage contrasting beautifully with the silvery-grey cardoon leaves, which are already towering above the salvia and nepeta. The courgette is a perfect form of huge, speckled leaves and the carrot tops are starting to emerge. I like to take a moment at this time of year to savour the garden. I suppose I should feel that the true beauty of a productive plot is when it's at its most productive, but I can't help being seduced by the perfection of the plants at this point of the growing season. Everything looks fresh and flawless; leaves haven't lost colour, stems haven't sagged under the burden of their crop and the scars of harvested leaves haven't appeared yet. There aren't any signs of bother-some pests, either. However, I've had a change of heart about my attitude towards pests in recent years. Growing organically is, first and foremost, a sensible position to take. If you're not obliterating them with noxious chemicals, it's probably wise to have a more pragmatic approach, as success rates take longer to achieve when you're using organic methods and there's no guarantee you'll eradicate them completely. Pests are a necessary evil, and not all of them are that bad. If you regard them as an essential part of a food chain, upon which all the other wildlife in your garden relies, you won't mind quite so much when the stems of your broad beans are covered in blackfly, or that as you sit down to enjoy a well-earned cup of tea, a company of cabbage white butterflies perform a delightful display as they flutter in and out of your brassicas. In the end, it's all about balance; some infestations are unsightly (blackfly and cabbage white caterpillars), but if dealt with quickly won't cause too

much damage or inhibit your plants' ability to produce a crop. Regularly check the undersides of brassica leaves and remove eggs or young caterpillars by hand to keep on top of the problem. Other pests create more havoc (for example vine weevils – see page 49) and it is worth spending a bit of time and effort in order to keep them at bay.

Aphids, or green and blackfly, are a good example of a pest that isn't too much of a pest. Left to their own devices, they work by smothering a plant's stem or bud in a thick blanket made up of hundreds of their tiny brethren. They breed incredibly quickly and feed on young, tender growth, leaving behind a sticky substance that attracts disease, which weakens the plant and can sometimes kill it. However the good news is that once you've spotted them, they're pretty easy to deal with. Best of all, they're the land equivalent of krill to all manner of insects. Aphids on your crops, and other pests for that matter, are all part of creating a balanced ecosystem, which will feed more than our hungry mouths. There's an award-winning 2018 documentary film called *The Biggest Little Farm*, which brilliantly explains this idea and shows that with more understanding and faith we can help nature restore harmony to our broken ecosystems. Obviously farmers are doing this on a big scale, but the principles are the same for any grower ... it's well worth watching.

Courgettes, blueberries and **beetroot**. For some, courgettes are a curse because they grow so vigorously – just one plant produces several courgettes a week. To me, this represents value for money and space. I love them roasted, sautéed and even grated and slowly cooked in garlic and butter, until it melts and becomes a rich sauce that I serve over pasta, grains or rice. In our house, blueberries tend to pep-up our morning cereals, but there's always the smoothie too!

APHID 101

DEPENDING ON THE SIZE of the infestation, you can wipe smaller clusters of aphids off plants, squishing them between your fingers. Alternatively, you can hose them off with a forceful jet of water.

A soapy solution, which can be homemade using a mix of water and an eco-friendly washing up liquid or vegetable oil, can be an effective method of suffocating the pests when applied with a spray bottle, but you need to cover them directly with the spray.

You can also treat with an insecticidal soap if you spot them. Simply dilute natural soap (or castile soap) in water and spray onto the plant. Try adding a couple of tablespoons of olive or sunflower oil to help the solution stick on the leaf for longer.

Natural predators are another environmentally friendly way to tackle the problem. Grow plants with berries, nectar or pollen to attract birds, earwigs, ladybirds, lacewings and hoverflies, who all feed on aphids. It isn't an overnight solution, but it introduces a balance in your garden that will help maintain a healthy ecosystem.

You can also buy biological controls, which are an organic way to control these pests using nematodes and other beneficial insects that feed on aphids or infect the pest with a fatal bacterial disease. Usually used in greenhouses, there are some, such as a small midge, green lacewing larvae, a parasitic wasp and a two-spotted ladybird, that can be used outdoors on aphids.

How to tackle aphids

June 23rd

Sweet potatoes

My green-fingered aunt warned me against growing sweet potatoes because it can be hard to get them to crop in our climate. She may well have a point (she has far more experience growing veg than I do). It was only six years ago that a farm in the south of England claimed they were the first to produce a British-grown variety that is frost resistant. Previous varieties from warm climates, typically south-eastern states of the USA, Egypt, Senegal and Israel, were grown here and were susceptible to cold temperatures, which affected yields and, ultimately, the health of the plants. Three years of challenging experimentation with a range of varieties resulted in success for Hill Farm in Kent – they grew them in raised beds covered with polythene, with a mulch-rich soil for warmer temperatures and regular watering via a drip. So, always up for a challenge and for the purposes of researching this book, I've decided to give them a go (despite a lack of polythene and automatic watering system), that, and the fact I came across some fantastically healthy looking plants in a local nursery, which, of course, I couldn't resist.

Bearing in mind it's mid June and the experts say you're looking for at least four or five months of warm weather for large yields, I feel slightly on the back foot. However, I'm planting a rooted slip (a shoot of a chitted potato), which in my book makes it about 3–4 weeks further down the line than I would be if I was planting a slip that hadn't produced roots yet. By my calculations, that takes me to the end of September – or four months give or take. It's going to be tight, and entirely dependent on having a glorious Indian summer at the end of the season. I'm also growing them in the greenhouse to give them as much warmth as possible. More by luck than judgement, I bought a variety called 'Beauregard', which was bred in 1987 and has since become the world's most popular variety of sweet potato, not to mention the most commonly grown in the UK. It's fast-maturing and performs well in our climate. I've also read that 'Carolina Ruby' is a good choice.

If you're buying slips that haven't been potted up yet, they might arrive looking a little limp – leave them in a glass of water overnight and they'll pick up again, ready to be planted in a small pots of multipurpose compost. Cover the whole length of the stem, right up to the base of the leaves, and place them somewhere warm to get established. Choose a large container and mix in plenty of grit to provide a free-draining soil. Make sure it has room to spread its vines, and as space is a bit tight in my greenhouse, I'm going to train it up several canes tied together like a teepee. Feed every two to three weeks with a high-potassium liquid feed and water regularly, ideally with tepid water.

Once the foliage starts to discolour at the end of summer, tubers should be ready to harvest. If you like super-sweet sweet potatoes, simply let them 'cure' or sit in a dark, cool, but not chilly, well-ventilated place for about two weeks. This also has the added benefit of toughening their

You say potato...

Its name in Haitian is batata, which filtered through Spanish as patata, giving rise to the word potato. During the sixteenth and seventeenth centuries it was brought back to Europe and considered an aphrodisiac, which possibly explains why in Shakespeare's *The Merry Wives of Windsor* (written in 1598), Falstaff, who is smitten with Mistress Ford, makes an otherwise foolish-sounding proclamation, 'Let the sky rain potatoes'. However, when the common potato gained popularity, the two had to be distinguished, hence its early name, Spanish potato, which became sweet potato by the end of the eighteenth century.

skin so they store for longer. Don't be tempted to go the whole hog and store them in the fridge (unless they've been cooked first), as it hardens the texture and ruins the flavour.

Enjoying superfood status (it contains more nutrients than spinach or broccoli, with higher levels of carotene, fibre and vitamin A, and lower amounts of carbohydrates and calories), sweet potato is also a good choice for diabetics because of its low glycaemic index, meaning that eating one does not cause a sudden spike in blood-sugar levels. Interestingly, it is also used as a type of fuel by several companies in Taiwan and as a dye in South America. Pedants of botany will appreciate that, being part of the morning glory family, sweet potatoes are a cousin to neither the common potato nor the yam.

Baby carrots and **courgettes**.

....

Lemon verbena. I remember a chef giving me the recipe for lemon verbena ice cream when I was writing my second book, *Kitchen Garden Experts*. I always find making ice cream a bit of a faff, but if you've not tasted lemon verbena flavour, it's worth the effort. Steven Doherty was the head chef at the George and Dragon in Cumbria at the time of researching the book, and this is his recipe (see overleaf).

Lemon verbena ice cream

(*Makes 1.5 litres*)
- 500ml milk
- Vanilla pod
- 100g granulated sugar

- 4 egg yolks
- 10 fresh lemon verbena leaves (finger-length)
- 500ml chilled double cream

Method

Combine the milk, vanilla seeds (scraped out of the pod), vanilla pod and half the sugar in a large saucepan and bring to just below boiling point. Remove from the heat, cover and let stand for at least 15 minutes to let the flavour develop.

Meanwhile, beat the egg yolks and remaining sugar in a heatproof bowl, until thick and pale. Bring the milk back to boiling point, then pour it on to the egg yolks and sugar, whisking steadily. Place the bowl over a saucepan of boiling water and stir the custard with a wooden spoon until it thickens. (You'll need to be patient – this can take up to half an hour … you see, faff!)

Remove from the heat, add the lemon verbena leaves and place in a large bowl of chilled water. Stir occasionally until the mixture is cool. Strain to remove the vanilla pod and lemon verbena leaves and transfer the custard and double cream into an ice-cream maker, or large plastic lidded box if, like me, you don't own one (chefs!).

Follow the ice-cream maker instructions or put the box into the freezer, remembering to take the box out and stir the mixture every half an hour or so, until it has the consistency of ice cream.

WEEKLY HARVEST

Courgette flowers. Funnily enough, Steven Doherty (of
the lemon verbena recipe) also swore by using pale ale and turmeric
to make a batter to coat these edible flowers. I like them, but Hal thinks
it's 'weird' to eat them. However, epicureans pay a lot of money for
fresh courgette flowers, so even if it's a short-lived fad, it's
worth harvesting them before they go over.

....

Broad beans, courgettes and **kale.** Broad bean hummus –
or dip – is my favourite way to eat them, even though it's fiddly, as you
have to remove both the pod and the skin of the bean. If you don't have
a huge harvest, bulk out the dip with dried fava beans. Puree the lightly
boiled broad beans (cook the dried fava beans as instructed), strain and
pour into a blender. Add crème fraiche, mint, and season. Buzz and
serve with crusty bread, or crunchy veg like raw carrots or radishes.

Sweet potatoes

Mollusc madness

The garden looks tired. The nepeta has gone over so I'm going to cut it back in the hope of a second flush. It'll still be worth it even if I'm a little late (the general advice is to cut back in early summer, which, if we're being precise, is June), because the faded, washed-out purple flowers that have flopped look sad and unloved (think a deflated air dancer figure, the type you see outside car sales forecourts). More to the point, it's a veritable hangout for the legions of lurking slugs and snails that wage relentless war on both crops and herbaceous plants, sending out troops each night to munch everything in the vicinity and then seem-

ingly vanishing when daylight comes. The glorious weather of April and May, with its searing temperatures and dry conditions, is all but a heady memory. It always surprises me how quickly I forget just how much damage these gastropods wilfully inflict on the garden in just a matter of hours. Unchecked, their assault is utterly soul destroying, and I can only urge you to conduct nightly searches to try to limit the carnage. Heavy rainfall and warm, muggy temperatures have created the perfect conditions to incubate them, resulting in a hive of activity as they ooze around the garden at the astonishingly effective speed of 1m per hour.

Ordinarily, I don't spend too much time considering slugs in any more depth than the damage they cause, but, after a little research for this book, I'm in awe of how successful these creatures are. Eating four times their body weight in the space of one evening sitting, they are able to stretch 20 times their length so that they become thin enough to squeeze through the smallest spot. Give them a red stretchy jump-suit and they could give Plastic Man of DC Comics fame a run for his money. Alarmingly, they have an unbelievable number of teeth – 27,000 apparently – and are hermaphroditic, so have a high strike-rate when it comes to producing offspring – theirs is not to worry about finding a suit-able soulmate. Though, if they do, they both become pregnant. It seems less surprising then, that it's believed any slug can have around 90,000 grandchildren, half of which, I can honestly say, are cruising around my flowerbeds every evening.

It's worth knowing your enemy when it comes to slugs, because leopard slugs, which in my experience grow to be absolutely massive, actually prefer fungi, organic or animal matter. In other words, these guys are a gardener's friend, keeping the garden clean and tidy as they gobble up dog poop (thank you), dead animals and decomposing vege-tation. They're less likely to be the culprits decimating your courgettes (leaves or crop), dahlias or anything in-between. That is the work of a large black variety with an eye-catching orange frill. The black slug is commonly found in gardens, and if you were to cut it in half, you'd see that it is mostly (your) plant foliage.

In terms of winning the war against slugs and snails, it really comes down to your general approach towards pest control in the garden. For those pure of heart and with plenty of time on their hands in the wee-small hours of the morning, you can't beat combing every inch of your garden to pick them off by hand, one by one. Wear a head torch to speed up the process and keep both hands free for lifting foliage and picking off. Slugs are much more disgusting to handle than snails, as their slime solidifies on your fingers within seconds – it's like an instant superglue and is really hard to wash off (a scrubbing brush is essential here). When Hal was young enough to find it fun rather than a chore, I used to tape plastic bags onto each of his hands and dispatch him into the garden with the challenge of finding 50 slugs and snails (he enjoyed it, honestly). Dispatching the spoils is an issue I find can cause a lot of consternation. Some fill buckets with water, others (and I won't name them as it sounds so brutal) chop them in half with secateurs, while I used to go for the gentler method of lobbing them into the then-derelict neighbour's garden. I hadn't realised that this was pretty ineffectual, as anything less than 20m won't be enough to tamper with their homing instinct (in the case of snails, or with slugs, a scent trail). It was a sad day when the house next door was bought and a lovely young couple moved in, leaving me with no choice but to rethink my method of getting rid of them (the slugs and snails, not the couple, obviously). In actual fact it did me a favour and the new method – emptying the bucket in the middle of the road outside my house, where they would either be squashed by a car or picked off by birds (or both) – is much more effective.

If you're not able to do this, growing plants with strong scents and hairy stems is said to deter them. I'm not 100 per cent sure about this, because I find the stems and leaves of courgettes hairy to the point of spikes, and yet they still seem to top the menu for slugs and snails. Rough surfaces, like egg shells, coffee grinds and gravel, are recommended deterrents, but in my experience they continue to happily slither across my shale. Another natural method is to encourage their predators, such as hedgehogs, ground beetles, rodents, slow worms and earthworms, into your garden – make sure hedgehogs can access your plot by leaving a gap in the fence for them to trundle in and out. There is a lot to be said for maintaining a balance and not interfering with the food chain too much. Then there are organic slug pellets, which poison snails and slugs (go for a brand that is safe for pets and birds), and wool fibre that clings to their slime and absorbs all their moisture. Salt is kryptonite to slugs and snails if you're not squeamish and happy to sprinkle it directly onto them.

Broad beans, courgettes, kale and **geranium** leaves. Kale crisps are great fun to make, and I've managed to tempt Hal with their salty, crispy flavour. I'm also making some botanical-infused gin to give as birthday presents to friends. First up, rose geranium vodka.

July 16th

Melons

I'm impatiently awaiting the moment when I am finally able to rig up an old bra in my greenhouse. Not, I assure you, in an attempt to horrify those neighbours who might be foolish enough to sneak a peek into my garden, nor to traumatise my son (though the ability to embarrass is, I understand, essential when parenting an 11-year-old). Rather it's because I'm told this is an old-fashioned method (albeit fairly

quirky) of supporting melons as they grow on the vine. Hang on. I've just read that back, and can honestly say the penny has only just dropped: I now see the connection between melons and bras. *Sighs*. I don't want to sound prudish, but the idea of making the fruit embody this metaphor seems more puerile than pure wit so I'm going to scrap the idea and find a few cloth bags to support them instead. (Let's see The Patriarchy make a sexist joke about that!) Alternatively, I've seen melon cradles available to buy online, which look like they'd do the job well, but they are made from industrial-grade plastic, so I'm happy to stick to a recycled solution.

Surprisingly, we have a long history of growing melons in this country. In the early 1700s, before glasshouses provided the necessary warmth and protection, gardeners relied on straw and rush matting to cover young plants when temperatures dropped. Stephen Switzer, a pioneer of the British landscape gardening movement, wrote numerous guides to growing fruit in the early eighteenth century, one of which is gloriously called *The Practical Kitchen Gardiner: Or, A New and Entire System of Directions For his Employment in the Melonry, Kitchen-garden and Potagery in the Several Seasons of the Year*. (Now that's a catchy title!) According to Switzer, the bar was set pretty high when it came to growing this fruit:

> ... owing to the correspondence that the nobility and gentry of
> Great Britain (that now equal, if not much excel the French and
> Dutch in their curious collections of feed) have abroad; but the
> second is owing to the industry and skill of our Kitchen Gardeners
> only, who are now behind no country in their performances.
> Heretofore it was counted a rare thing to cut melons by the middle
> of June, or perhaps the latter end, tho' now the latter end of
> April, or beginning of May is the season for the first crop.

Melon mania reached its heights during the Victorian era, when landed gentry with more money than sense built special glasshouses and positively encouraged their head gardeners to get one over on their neighbours in the stately home nearby by breeding a 'house' variety of melon, which had characteristics favoured by the family. I can only assume these were based on flavour. Two examples, both of which were developed on Oxfordshire estates in the 1800s, are 'Blenheim Orange', a delicious orange-fleshed fruit, and the smaller, yellow 'Hero of Lockinge'.

Although melons were traditionally grown in heated greenhouses, some new varieties can be grown outside, but I've only ever grown cantaloupe melons in my (unheated) greenhouse. In the main, experts conclude that our climate is too unpredictable for outdoor growing and, as melons need plenty of sunshine, failing a long, hot summer, a warm corner somewhere that also has a bit of humidity is the next best thing. You might try them in the house on a south-facing windowsill, though I imagine it might be a bit of a squeeze because they need a decent-sized container. A better idea might be in front of an outside door (if it's glass) or on a sheltered balcony. If starting from seed rather than a plug plant, soak for 12 hours or so to help soften the coating and encourage germination. Sow a couple of seeds in each 9cm pot and cover with clingfilm to heat things up a little. When seedlings are large enough to handle, repot in the next size pot and when it's time to transplant into the final container, mix a bit of grit into the compost because they need plenty of water but don't like sitting in waterlogged soil. Add three or four canes for the vines to climb up, tying together with string to form a tripod support, feed regularly throughout the growing season, and if you want big fruit, some form of bottom heat is essential. As mentioned, they like a bit of humidity too, which can attract aphids, so keep an eye on the underside of the leaves (see page 187 for aphid control methods).

Once the flowers have set, choose one fruit and remove the others, as less is more when it comes to growing melons and a sweet, fleshy fruit is better than lots of bland smaller ones. The whole net/bag issue comes in because you want to wait for the melon to drop off the vine before harvesting, so as the fruit swells, get ready to rig up whatever it is you're using for support. A quick internet search suggests home-made hammocks too, though I fear we're straying back into bra territory. Essentially, melons need some sort of support so feel free to make your choice. Judgement free.

Courgettes, **kale** and **cucumber**. Pickled cucumber is our homemade addition to veggie burgers, which is easy to do as these days quick pickles seem all the rage. Slice two cucumbers thinly, cover with 2 tbsp of white wine vinegar, 1 tbsp of caster sugar and chopped dill and/or mustard seeds.

....

Currants. Hal makes a super-tasty, quick flapjack-type tray bake – combining our redcurrants, sugar, oats and cinnamon. The key to making this totally fantastic is the pureed date and apple middle layer. However, I think it can be tweaked to suit the seasons, and as we tend to find currants a bit sharp to eat raw, slightly cooking them with raspberries or blueberries and spreading between the oaty layers makes for a delicious and relatively healthy snack.

Melons

Celeriac

Gardening is good for the mind, body and soul. A connection with nature, which our grandparents would have enjoyed far more readily (and possibly our great-grandparents) is something that many of us are only able to wistfully imagine. What better antidote to the daily pressures and pace of our life than finding the time to observe a bee as it potters in and out of pollen-laden flowers, or noticing the new buds of a plant as it emerges from the soil? While Hal's watch alerts him when it is time for him to stop and relax (I mean, really?), I much prefer to let nature set the pace and to willingly adjust to her soothing rhythms.

I also think another much-underrated benefit of gardening is how it mirrors the pattern of life. The simple act of sowing a seed is imbued with a sense of hope and excitement to see it develop and grow, producing a crop or mature plant. However, despite the very best of intentions and often faultless garden practice, 100 per cent success rates aren't guaranteed. Try as you might, sometimes other forces are at work and a plant can be eaten overnight (see slugs and snails) or a crop produces a lacklustre bounty. Yet Mother Nature presses on. There is always next season, another opportunity to give it a go. Before you know it, you're back in the saddle and marvelling at this year's success stories, and not minding quite so much about the losses.

So, it is with this spirit of acceptance and optimism that I only felt mild irritation that my second planting of peas failed (again, I refer you to the entry on slugs and snails). It's too late for me to try again, but I really want to fill the gap that was opened up when I cut back the sweet cicely at the end of May after it finished flowering (and have been rewarded with lush foliage that will look fresh until the first frosts). There are three dahlias in the bed already (I planted them last year to give the bed some late autumn colour for a *Gardeners' World* magazine shoot), and they're a welcome addition, even though the slugs and snails are doing their very best to demolish them entirely. The artichoke leaves at the base of the plant have also been nibbled and look old, so I've removed them (this also allows some air to circulate in the bed and removes hiding places for pests, like, yes, you've guessed it, slugs and snails). The fennel is now putting its energy into producing its beautiful mustard-coloured flowers rather than new growth. Peas climbing and twining up hazel poles would have looked great and perfectly filled the gap, but I need to rethink the possibilities.

My solution is celeriac, the delicious cousin of celery. It's perfect, as it can still be planted out in July to get the benefit of the summer months, though don't let it dry out as it has shallow roots that need plenty of moisture, and will put on plenty of feathery growth. Depending on the summer, I can expect a crop in October, which can be stored in boxes of sand in a frost-free location – so a garage, greenhouse or cupboard under the stairs is ideal. You can also leave them in the ground if you're not too exposed, which I find preferable. I need to order some poultry manure pellets (or ask my friends with chickens for a scoop or two of chicken manure), which will provide the necessary nutrients. Other than removing the lower leaves to reveal the crown of the plant and help the bulb (the edible part, though horticulturally speaking, this part is actually a swollen stem) to develop, there's very little else it needs in the way of care.

I have grown on plugs of 'Giant Prague', a tasty heirloom variety that dates back to the late 1800s when it was developed in Germany and then became popular in France (where it was and is made into the delicious remoulade) and America. My choice is largely because in 'lockdown', this was the variety available from the seed company from which I had managed to secure an order (believe me, no mean feat ... think the tension surrounding the Glastonbury Festival ticket hotline at 7 a.m. when the lines open).

Earlier, when I had an allotment in London, I grew 'Prinz', because my elderly allotment neighbour was still offering a ready supply of advice for me as I was clearly such a novice. He advocated disease-resistant varieties, much in the way my grandparents' generation embraced chemical feeds and poisons to maintain control over their plants. To him, stronger, healthier plants were the key. 'Prinz' promised to resist the urge to bolt and set seed, as well as withstand the viral infections that would damage its leaves. I did and do see his point. As you'll read throughout this book, growing fruit and vegetables organically is largely a case of one step forward, two steps back to begin with, while you find your feet and your garden finds it's natural balance (for a masterclass in the subject, I refer, once again, to the documentary *The Biggest Little Farm*). It's not wrong to choose more resilient varieties to boost better harvests, but I lean towards flavour over bulletproof varieties, after all, much of the reason for growing your own fruit and veg is to enjoy how much better it tastes when compared with shop-bought alternatives. I'm looking forward to trying my 'Giant Prague', which is noted for its pronounced celery flavour, and will try 'Alabaster' in the future – another variety with great flavour.

If you are daunted by the knobbly exterior and put off by the inevitable waste in peeling celeriac, try 'Monarch' or 'Brilliant', which have been bred for their smooth skin, as well as, I'm told, great flavour. If size is your thing, 'Mars' (clearly ironically named as it's the second-smallest planet in the solar system) produces the largest bulbs.

Raspberries and a **marrow**, discovered hidden under leaves. Home-grown raspberries don't last long in our house as they are picked and then eaten seconds later. In homage to my mum, I've opted for the gloriously old-fashioned recipe of stuffed marrow (with packet sage and onion stuffing) served with veggie sausages.

Propagation techniques

Saving seed is an easy way to get plants for free, but for some shrubs you'll need to take cuttings from the parent plant. It may sound more complicated, but it's just another way to bulk up your own plant stocks or have them on hand to give to friends and family, so it's well worth having a go. You'll need a pair of sharp secateurs and some small pots with potting compost and perlite (to improve soil structure).

Over the next couple of months, you can take cuttings from herbs like bay (via heel cutting, where the branching part and a strip of stem are cut away), lavender (June–September), rosemary, sage and thyme as well as bushes like gooseberries and black, red and whitecurrants.

Taking cuttings: a snip, a dip, and you're away...

1. Choose a healthy stem and remove the soft, new leaf growth at the tip, snipping cleanly above a bud at the top. Make sure this top cut is at an angle to help water run off the cutting.

2. You'll want to take a 15cm-long section for herbs and smaller bushes, or a slightly longer 25cm section for larger shrubs. Make a straight cut at the bottom of the cutting, just below a pair of buds or a leaf junction.

3. Dip the bottom of the cutting in hormone rooting powder, which helps promote root growth and prevents it from rotting, and insert into a pot filled with soil so that the top one-third of the cutting is above the surface of the soil.

4. Allow about 10cm between cuttings and place somewhere sheltered and out of direct sunlight until the following autumn, when they can be potted on.

5. Keep an eye on them, particularly over the summer, so they don't dry out.

Grab your bread knife and use a bit of elbow grease

To ensure perennials like asters, Japanese anemones, heuchera and sedum remain strong and healthy so they can put on a show year after year, it's a good idea to lift and divide them every four or five years. Loosen the soil around the root system, taking care not to damage any roots, and lift the plant. Gently brush soil away so you can see the root system and any buds forming at the base. If the root ball isn't too big, you can use a bread knife to cut it in half; if it's too big use two forks, placed back to back, to tease the root system apart. If you can divide into more sections, repeat the process, but you'll need to make sure there's a bud in each division. Remove the old woody growth from the divisions too, and then replant at the same depth as the original plant. Make sure you water well, straight after planting, to help the roots re-establish themselves. If you don't want all the divisions in your garden, pot them up in containers, tie a bow around them and give them away to friends!

Lettuce and **courgettes**. Slow-roast courgettes in plenty of olive oil with garlic, so they are soft and unctuous, and serve with mozzarella, or burrata if you feel like treating yourself, topped with lots of salt and black pepper.

....

Tomatoes. I also tried drying a handful of cherry tomatoes to top our pizzas – I was worried about flies, so didn't try this in the heat of the day, rather in the oven at its lowest temperature. I cut them in half, sprinkled a little olive oil and salt over them, and left them in the oven for just over two hours. Keep an eye on them so you take them out when they're soft and chewy, rather than too dry.

Watering – water butts, watering systems and recycled water

A common theme throughout this book is my rather erratic approach to watering. I'm not proud of it, and it's something I'm constantly trying to address. The principle is that vegetables in beds and borders should be encouraged to put down a strong network of roots to provide sufficient water throughout the growing seasons. The theory is, if you water them too much, you'll spoil them, with the result that they have a smaller root system and ultimately are at risk from becoming weak and unhealthy. I tend to find that this

is the case, especially for perennial veg, though I do have a good success rate with my border-grown crops, which have deeper roots as a result of not being overwatered. On the other hand, container-grown plants are almost completely reliant on our help – they can't put down their roots to reach a natural water source as crops in the ground do, and a shower of rain doesn't always provide enough water because their leaves may be too dense to let enough water trickle down into

the soil. As a general rule, smaller pots dry out more quickly than larger ones. If in doubt, check that the compost is not dry, and in hot weather be prepared to water containers once, sometimes twice, a day. That said, overwater your plants and you'll most likely cause leaves to wilt or the plant to die. The best way to avoid this is to make sure that the pot has sufficient drainage, with holes in the bottom of the container.

To ensure that plants have water right where it's needed (in other words, at their roots), insert an upturned plastic tube or bottle with the bottom cut off, and fill this each time you water. This way, water is delivered directly to the plants' roots as opposed to the surrounding compost. It's also worth adding a layer of mulch, like decorative gravel, to containers to help retain moisture. You can use more robust mulches, like bark, well-rotted manure and gravel with a higher diameter in borders and beds.

If you're using a watering can, take the rose off when watering in beds, borders or in containers to direct a steady flow of water to the roots rather than spraying the foliage. However, always use a rose when watering young seedlings or delicate plants, to prevent them from getting damaged by the weight of water being poured on them.

If you are going away on holiday and can't persuade a friend to water your plants, it's worth trying either water-retaining granules or a watering system, which are much easier to install than you might imagine.

During the summer months when rain can be in short supply and hosepipe bans can be imposed, saving water from the sink and baths is a sensible idea, though that depends on using organic soap and other cleaning products, especially on edible crops. Alternatively, and if you have space, a water butt is a good idea too (check to see if your local council offers subsidised water butt kits).

Courgettes, **kale** and **tomatoes** added to pasta, **cucumber** and **lettuce** in wraps for lunch and **lemon verbena** ice cream as a treat.

....

Chard and **plums** from a friend. A lovely brunch of scrambled eggs with lightly sautéed chard. We had so many plums I made crumble, as well as jam, and we even had enough for a few slow-roasted in a bit of white wine and honey with cinnamon, to eat with ice cream.

....

Tomatoes and foraged **blackberries**. A couple of beefsteak tomatoes were ready, and surprisingly tasty. Hal ate his plain, while I sprinkled mine with balsamic vinegar, olive oil and basil leaves … soaking up the juice with some fresh bread. We also picked blackberries this week. They were still a little too tart to eat raw, so we made jam with them.

....

Sweetcorn. I managed to harvest several mini cobs, which I blanched and then finished-off on the BBQ and served with plenty of butter and salt. I have left a few on the plant to grow a bit bigger – I'm hoping for 20cm when fully mature – so that I can dry them on the kitchen counter and when the kernels are hard, I can make popcorn for Hal and I.

Now the garden is in full swing, producing plenty of tasty treats, it's the perfect time to sit back and relax. Other than watering, feeding and keeping an eye on pests, there's precious little to do, so make the most of your time. Sit in the garden if you can, to watch the insects and creatures you've created habitats for, and make plans for next year's beds and containers – more lettuce, fewer courgettes, perhaps! If you're going on holiday, make sure you suggest that friends or neighbours feel free to harvest whatever is ripe and ready, as a thank you for their help and to keep plants as productive as possible.

Autumn

Make medlar jam, quince cheese, sloe gin, etc.

Harvest pumpkins.

Collect leaves – store behind the shed in hessian sacks.

Save seeds.

Make compost.

Tidy greenhouse.

Sow basil, dill, chives and parsley on a windowsill. Try pea shoots
for a fresh flavour during wintry months.

Direct-sow winter hard pea 'Meteor' and broad beans for spring, as
well as sweet peas. Sweet peas are worthwhile sowing now to get ahead
next year – lovely in pots, they're such happy guests at the veg party.

Sow onions for a June harvest.

Plant bulbs – garlic and tulips.

Pot up wild, self-sown seedlings.

Remove larger unripened figs. Counterintuitive as it might seem,
if your figs have unripened fruit on them, best remove them as they
won't ripen in spring – better that the tiny fruits are left and can benefit
from the plant's energy next spring to produce a good harvest.

Kale

I really should (and would like to) spend an afternoon pottering about in the garden. It needs a gentle tidy-up, nothing too severe as a bit of a messy plot provides a des-res for all manner of wildlife. However, the holidays have finished and I've just started working on a new garden TV show, so time is a bit short. I nip out at lunchtime (which, as any freelancer will tell you, is a moveable feast at best, though more often than not nonexistent) and scrape away the dead catnip stems so that I can plant a couple of the 'Black Magic' cavolo nero grafted plugs that arrived yesterday (I wanted to give them the best chance of withstanding the darn slugs and snails), along with the purple sprouting broccoli and some leeks, and find space for the rest of them in the other beds. I'm amazed to see two other cavolo nero plants, which I planted earlier in the season and are complete stars despite being thoroughly neglected. I had also wanted to pop some garlic into the beds for early summer cropping – wet garlic is delicious, but I don't have time so it will have to wait until another time. (Probably November, which is actually often thought of as the best month to plant it.)

The curly kale is looking incredible – it's such a versatile

plant, and in addition to being edible, it has a structural habit that adds a bit of drama to the border, especially as other plants start to fade and die back. It's my all-time favourite crop, providing a regular harvest of new, tender growth, which is easy to pick and isn't covered in protein-rich caterpillar snacks. Friends love it too and a few have said they're going to try it in their own plots next year, even though they don't usually grow veg. I'm also pleased with the celery, and celeriac, which is adding lush foliage to the plot and is working well as underplanting for the myrtle in the large container. In this pot I combined it with thyme, and have planted it in another pot with rainbow chard. I've had to brush off the myrtle flowers, which are covering the area in a blanket of petals.

The strawberry tree has produced a small crop of fruit (it did better last year), but I've noticed some buds too. Quite apart from it being an elegant, small tree – perfect for a small city plot – it adds interest to the garden when other trees have blossomed or fruited. It's a lovely addition.

Kale and the last of the **tomatoes** to add to a minestrone soup. **Lettuce** to add crunch to Hal's packed lunch wrap, and **chilli** – well, to liven up lots of dishes.

Chilean guava

I've just nipped into the garden for some bay leaves, and as soon as I opened the back door was hit by the heady scent of my container-grown Chilean guava. It's so heavenly, I couldn't resist stopping for a moment to breathe deeply and try to come up with the words that best describe it: bubble gum, honey. I realise this sounds sickly, but it's more floral than saccharine, which elevates it into an utterly divine fragrance, especially on a warm, balmy evening.

An evergreen shrub, it provides pretty pink blossom followed by plum-red berries, which really do brighten up a wintry garden. Said to be Queen Victoria's favourite fruit, they contain five times the amount of vitamin C in an orange and have high levels of iron too.

I grow mine in a container, but if it's in the ground, make sure to give it moist, free-draining soil in either full sun or partial shade. I've found that it's really hardy and has endured fairly harsh winters, so I'm confident recommending it for all but the coldest, wettest region without any winter protection (don't forget, my walled garden is fairly sheltered). It has been in the same decent-sized pot since I bought it about four years ago, so I think it's time to repot, or at least scrape off a layer of soil and refresh it with new soil to give it a nutritional boost. It can also be grown as a hedge, which I think sounds delightful – I'd definitely do that if I had more space.

I've made muffins and jelly from the berries, and in Chile they're made into pies and jellies, but you can be a bit more creative by cooking with apples to make fruit leathers. There are some delicious recipes online that suggest slightly crushing berries in a litre of vodka with some orange peel, or making a version of the traditional Chilean liqueur Murtado, which as far as I can tell is made by steeping the berries in brandy and sweetening with syrup for a few weeks.

Beetroot, to make Ottolenghi's delicious beetroot hummus; roasted **peppers** added to pasta; **grapes**, which lasted about five minutes; and **lemon verbena** tea.

Garlic chives

Mum sent me some garlic chives today. She's grown this herb for years, but as it was getting a bit unruly, she's lifted and divided it to encourage strong, healthy growth next year. If you love garlic, this pretty, evergreen herb is a must for your plot as it provides a fresh supply of garlic-flavoured leaves all year round. Bees and other beneficial insects love the nectar-rich flowers too, so when it's in bloom during June to August, your garden will be filled with a blissful buzzing sound. It can be grown on windowsills, too. March and April are the best months to start seeds off in 5cm pots under cover. When seedlings are stronger, plant out in a border or container, in rich, moist but well-drained soil. Choose a sunny spot for best results, though it will put up with some shade. Pick leaves all year round to provide tasty culinary treats, as well as keep the plant in good health. Its white flowers are edible and make a lovely addition to salads during summer months. Harvesting them also helps intensify the flavour in leaves.

I blanched the **kale** leaves, as this way they can be frozen and kept for up to six months to be used in soups and smoothies; **cucumber** and **tomato** salad; **lettuce** leaves added to lentil salad; and sautéed grated **courgette** as a pasta sauce.

September 23rd

Repotting

Most indoor or outdoor container-grown perennial plants will eventually outgrow their pots – the telltale sign being a mass of roots escaping from the drainage holes. You might also notice that the soil dries out quickly or, if you're able to lift the plant out of the pot, its roots are tightly packed together with little or no spare soil. It's easy to resolve by choosing a slightly bigger pot and transplanting the plant. Now, in a spectacular example of do as I say, not as I do, I threw caution to the wind this morning and rashly decided to repot my cardamom. Strictly speaking, spring is the best time to repot plants, which makes sense because they'll be coming out of their dormant period so won't be too shocked by the abrupt change of home. That said, I couldn't help feeling there was no time like the present when I was moving the plant back into the greenhouse for the winter, and I'm fairly confident that it will cope – in fact I'm hoping it will thank me in the shape of a spectacular display of new growth next year.

In the main, I like my plants to be rough and ready ... I don't have much time (metaphorically or literally) for tender specimens, and there's nothing more soul-destroying than seeing something struggle and fail as a result of your care (or lack thereof). However, for some odd reason I fell in love with the cardamom plant I bought in a pot online, which needs a bit more in the way of care than other plants in my plot. Misting for a start, which, you won't find hard to believe, is a bit hit and miss as to how often I do it, and I wouldn't dream of leaving it outside once the temperature starts to drop. My plant is three years old now and I think I should have repotted it last year. In its native southern India, it can reach heights of up to 2m before it flowers and produces its fragrant seeds,

Repotting

so I'm just over a metre and a half off. While I'd love to be able to sample this harvest, I'm content with the intoxicatingly spicy citrus scent that fills the greenhouse in spring and the garden during the summer months.

Repotting plants is a satisfying job, though it can be awkward if the roots have seemingly adhered to the sides and bottom of the pot, or the shape narrows at the top or has a lip, all of which requires a bit of judicious poking and pressing to overcome the physical problem of a large mass passing through a smaller circumference. If you do encounter issues, loosen the soil around the top edges and remove as much excess as you can. Then try either turning it upside down and easing it out with sharp downward jolts, or, if it's too big to handle in this way, try knocking the pot against a bench, being careful not to break the pot. For really stubborn plants, I've had to cut around the edge of the pot with a knife and pull hard. Before you replant, check the roots and remove damaged or unhealthy-looking sections. Tightly packed roots don't do their job properly, so using secateurs or a knife, gently cut sections around the root ball and carefully open up the tangled root system with your fingers. Repot in the usual way, with a good, soilless compost that covers the top of the root ball by about 2cm.

Chillies, peppers and our **melon**, which, if I'm honest, wasn't as juicy and delicious as I'd hoped. I think watering could have been an issue ... I'm going to try again next year. I steeped a few chillies in oil to use on pasta and lentil dishes, and dried a couple of handfuls, simply threading them through the tops with a needle and thread, so that I could hang them to slowly shrivel up, ready to be chopped and used throughout the winter. We used the pepper as a pizza topping.

....

A few **apples**, which we chopped and added to a sponge cake, and, of course, made an apple crumble!

Spinach

If I could, I would eat spinach every day. I know for some it's just too slimy and unappetising, but I absolutely adore its slightly wilted leaves in everything from scrambled eggs to saag paneer. Tender baby leaves are best, but I find it's easy to end up with spinach running to seed as soon as it hits a dry spell and it's not watered sufficiently. Thankfully I discovered perpetual spinach, also known as spinach beet, which isn't quite so pernickety and copes perfectly well in hot weather. It's also a biennial, so in a belt-and-braces approach to choosing your variety, this spinach

won't even try to go to seed until it's the second growing season. Part of the chard family, it more than earns its place in my veg patch (and sometimes containers) as it provides a bounty pretty much all year round. It's perfectly happy in a sunny or partially shady spot, and is more vigorous than spinach, though you do need to keep on top of weeds.

Sow this spinach all year round, but if you want to use it to fill the hunger-gap months, sow in early autumn for a winter harvest, or between March and April for early summer pickings. Sow thinly directly into the soil, about 3cm deep and in rows about 30cm apart, or scatter over soil in a container, covering with another 3cm of soil. You can pick small, tender leaves to use as a salad leaf or let them get a little larger for cooking. However, a good rule of thumb is to harvest 7–8 weeks after sowing, picking the outer leaves first. Always pick leaves that are ready, to keep the plant producing new young leaves. If you can't use them fresh, make a delicious spinach pesto and freeze to use later on.

Pumpkin and **chilli** for a warming autumn soup, **chard**, and, yes, it turns out my aunt did have a point when it came to **sweet potatoes** – mine didn't produce anything worth shouting about (or roasting for that matter). That said, and it's confession time, I did let the container dry out a few too many times and this will have certainly arrested their development ... I didn't use tepid water when watering them either, but I did provide an otherwise good environment for them: planting them in a huge container in my greenhouse. If the vines that entwined my rake and spade handles were anything to go by, it looked like they were more than happy. But I didn't feed them as much as I should have either. I might try again next year and pay more attention in the aftercare stakes.

Seed saving

The veg plot is no longer groaning with produce, but pumpkins, cabbage and even salads provide a welcome crop, and it's a good time to refuel empty beds by sowing green manures like phacelia, winter tares and crimson clover. And, if you want to bulk up stocks of a

favourite vegetable or ornamental, now's the time to collect seed from a range of varieties. Choose plants that are strong and healthy as they're likely to have good-quality seed, however be aware if they're hybrids (specially bred plants that are unlikely to have the same qualities as the parent plant) rather than species, the seed won't 'come true' from seed – your best bet is to either buy new plants the following year or be prepared for the seeds to produce something

completely different, which sounds like fun to me.

Start off by deciding which plants you're saving seed from because some require different techniques. Tomatoes, peppers, beans, peas and pumpkins are a good place to start as they're very simple to save.

Collecting seeds from tomatoes and berries is a bit messy, but well worth the effort. Harvest the fruit before the birds have a chance to eat them all and mash them in a fine sieve so you can rinse away the pulp from the seeds. Dry the seeds over a day or two by laying them out on paper towels. Don't forget that seeds and berries are an important food source for birds during the cold winter months so leave some on the plant – there's plenty to go around!

For larger varieties like peppers, chillies, aubergines, courgettes, pumpkins and squashes, cucumbers and melons, cut them open and pick out the seeds, clean if necessary and dry on paper towels.

For peas and all types of bean, leave a few to mature and dry on the bush, then pick and remove the seeds. As they need to be really dry to store, try pushing a fingernail into the skin, and if it leaves a dent, place them somewhere warm and dry before storing.

Beetroot, chard, basil, coriander, dill, broccoli, kale, Brussels sprouts, mizuna, pak choi, lettuce and rocket leaves will all send up a flower stem and go to seed if left unharvested. The trick is to collect seed just before it's dispersed. It's a bit of a waiting game, but once the seed head has ripened and changed colour (from green to brown, black or red) and is dry and crisp, it's time to leap into action. Place seed heads in a separate paper bag (one for each species) or, if they'll come away easily, place a paper bag over the seed head and gently shake. Parsley and carrots are biennial, meaning they will flower in the second year, so if you have space, leave a few carrots in the ground and collect the seeds the following season. Once you've gathered all the seeds you want, lay them out on a warm windowsill or on a greenhouse bench – you can even find a spot in the airing cupboard. You want to give them time to dry out so you can get to the seed more easily. Clean away the 'chaff' or casing so you're left with just the seed.

It's immensely satisfying transferring your seeds into individual paper packets and labelling them. Keep them together in an airtight container and if you have any sachets of silica gel from new shoes or bags, place a couple in with the seeds to absorb excess moisture, which would otherwise cause the seeds to rot. If not, add a handful or two of rice into the container and find a spot for them in the fridge. It's also important to label your seeds, including the name, variety and date you collected them – if you're anything like me, you'll be surprised how quickly you forget what's what, and it's also helpful if you want to swap seeds with friends and family.

Cavolo nero and **kale**, added to a lemon and ricotta cheese lasagne.

....

Pickings were thin on the ground this week, so we made do
with **herbs** to brighten up a few home-cooked dishes.

Tidying up

Another wet and dreary morning, with no sign of brightening up. My hybrid tea rose, 'Chartreuse de Parme', dahlias and purple top verbena all add pops of magenta, which stand out from the rain-soaked greens.

I've harvested the sweetcorn but can't face consigning the plant to the compost – it looks a bit tired, but beautiful, and the fading leaves bring a bit of height and interest to the garden. While most of the plants have begun to fade, others enjoy their moment in the spotlight – the cavolo nero and chard, for example. These winter stalwarts do need a bit of TLC to get them through the harsher weather. I've mounded up the soil around their bases, to anchor them more securely in the ground and protect their roots, which are easily damaged with too much movement, and staked the kale and sprouts for the same reason. You can eat the leafy tops of your Brussels sprouts now as it won't affect the plant – the sprouts will wait patiently to be picked for Christmas. I also removed dead leaves and any that were starting to turn yellow – if they're left to slowly decompose on the plant, they can encourage fungal disease and create the perfect environment for pests to flourish. Try and keep a lid on cabbage whitefly and mealy cabbage aphid (see page 186), which really can get a grip over the summer and then hang out over the winter to hit the ground running again in spring.

I will cover the globe artichokes with a thick layer of mulch to help protect them, and if you have cauliflower in your plot (I don't), use a couple of their leaves to protect their curds (the white heads themselves), covering the curds with the adjacent leaves like a hood and securing them in place at the top with string.

As soon as there's a break in the weather I need to take the wooden containers into the greenhouse, otherwise they'll start to rot over the winter. I will also move the now-empty terracotta pots and put a brick (though you can use special pot feet if you're feeling like splashing a bit of cash) under the other terracotta pots that are too heavy to move, to lift them off the ground.

Sweetcorn ... eaten two ways! The mini corn was a little drier than I'd hoped, so I'll try again and make more effort to keep it well watered. As Hal likes sweetcorn, I didn't want to do anything too fussy, so quickly boiled it and smothered it in butter, salt and pepper. We set two corns aside to dry for making popcorn.

Show the birds and bees you care too...

My plot is one of 25 back-to-back gardens in the three streets that make up a T-shaped row of Victorian terraced houses. Based on this number, I'm willing to bet there are at least 25 cats. We have two for starters, and I know of three other households, each with two cats, so that has to cancel out the non-cat owners. This absolutely rules out putting up any bird boxes or providing food to coax birds into the garden. As it is, I worry about the sweet pair of pigeons who find the amelanchier's bounty of juicy berries irresistible in June, and a male blackbird who is tempted by the myrtle berries. Full disclosure: one of our cats is a rather large lady and I suspect she would require a combination of crampons and oxygen to climb a tree in pursuit of an extra meal – although that's assuming she could muster the energy and will in the first place. Our other cat is too clumsy to pose a threat. He's so enthusiastic that he spends most of his time falling off branches and sliding off the narrow fence, which thankfully means we haven't had to deal with unwanted gifts. (The same can't

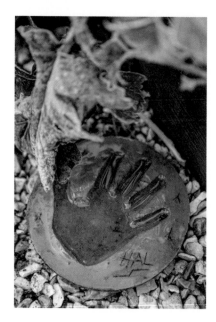

Fat cakes

You'll need one-part fat (suet or lard) to two-parts dry ingredients (wild bird seed, currants, sultanas, oats, cake crumbs and bread). Melt the fat in a saucepan and pour over the mixture of dry ingredients. Make a hole in the base of a yoghurt pot and thread through a length of twine. Fill the pots with the mixture and allow to set in the fridge overnight. Cut the pot to remove the fat cake, tie a knot in the twine to secure the fat cake in place, and hang up in a tree or shrub.

be said for a rather thuggish pair of moggies, who live at number 12. Just kidding, neighbour!)

However, I've made more than my fair share of fat balls for various magazine features and wanted to share a simple recipe that you can make if the birds in your garden don't have feline foes to contend with. Fat cakes are an ideal food source for all sorts of birds, and can be made using kitchen leftovers. When it's cold and wet outside, garden birds can really use this extra boost to give them energy and keep them warm.

Kale and leeks to make a flan, a couple of **Brussels sprouts** sliced and sautéed with other green veg, and **medlars**.

Show the birds and bees you care too...

November 10th

Share the love

It's hard to beat homemade gifts, especially the edible ones. While flashy presents have their place, what's not to like about a jar of home-made marmalade or a slab of this season's quince cheese. (I do realise I appear to have hit the jackpot with my group of friends, who all produce deli-style treats.)

I must confess, I haven't always felt this way. In my student days, my granny's friend used to send me jars of dark brown vegetable chutney. It was so kind of her, but it looked thoroughly unappetising and I'm ashamed to say the jars were left, untouched at the back of the cupboard. Now that I have spent afternoons making jams and chutneys to give to my own friends and family, I feel differently about this sort of gift. (Assuming the recipe is chosen with care and everything passes a taste test – if you wouldn't eat it, why should anyone else?) It's hard to find a more personal or thoughtful gift, and if it's home-grown, so much the better. I love the whole process, from picking (if possible) and preparing the ingredients to designing the labels. I have no idea if my homemade gifts are devoured within a week or end up languishing on a shelf, but these days I'm firmly in the camp that believes 'it's the thought that counts'.

While your garden is a great place to find ingredients, if it's small, you might not have enough spare produce. Don't despair: do as I do, and head off into your neighbourhood to take advantage of any unwanted spoils.

Earlier today I popped to a house a couple of streets away that has a gnarly old medlar tree in the front garden. Two years ago I knocked on the door to ask if the owners would be happy for me to pick a few dozen fruits in exchange for a jar of the jam I was hoping to make. I'm thrilled to say this arrangement still stands, because ugly as these fruits are (they're nicknamed dog's arse fruit, need I say any more?), they make the most delicious, delicately flavoured preserve. Medlars aren't huge trees, but there are now patio-sized varieties available (try 'Sibley's Patio Medlar'), which reach about 1.5–2m in height – great news if you're in the market for a container-grown compact specimen, or have a small gap in a border. As with all trees, autumn is a good time to plant them so that they can get

Medlar jelly

- 2.5kg bletted medlars, washed and halved
- 3 lemons, washed and cut into quarters

- 900g granulated sugar
- 2 litres of water

Method

Pour the water into a heavy-bottomed saucepan, add the medlars and lemons and simmer until the medlars are mushy. Transfer into a large sieve lined with muslin and leave the liquid to drip through overnight. It's important to resist the urge to squeeze or press the fruit at any point, as this will make your jelly cloudy.

Measure the juice and tip into a clean saucepan – add 450g sugar for every 650ml of juice. Stir over a low heat until the sugar has dissolved and then boil rapidly, without stirring, until it's at setting point. (To test if it's at setting point, chill a saucer in the fridge, spoon a blob of the liquid onto it and return to the fridge for a couple of minutes. Push your finger through the chilled liquid and if it wrinkles, it has reached setting point. If not, continue boiling and repeat the process until it wrinkles.)

Pour into warm, sterilised jars and seal immediately. It will keep unopened for up to a year and should be refrigerated after opening.

established before the weather warms. They'll cope in all soil types and as long as they have a bit of sun, will produce a welcome harvest from October – around 30 fruits by the time the tree is four years old. Ideally don't pick the fruits until after the first frosts, which bletts them (or turns them soft and brown). It might sound unpleasant, but it improves their flavour no end. If you're not able to do this, leave foraged or shop-bought fruits on a plate somewhere cool, until they soften.

It's also quince season, but I have to go further afield to gather a stash – thankfully my parents have a kindly neighbour with a magnificent quince slap-bang in the centre of their perfectly manicured lawn. A modest 2kg supply makes 1.5kg of quince cheese, which is a lovely festive gift. Thanks to the same fruit experts, 'Sibley's Patio Quince' has also

been bred to appeal to those of us with small gardens. Disease resistant, this variety will reach about 1.2m in height and produce a whopping 50 fruits when it's three years old.

Don't forget to forage sloes, too – Christmas isn't the same without sloe gin, and rose hips can make a deliciously sweet syrup.

Quince cheese (or membrillo)

Full disclosure: this is a labour of love – there's no other way of saying it – but it's totally worth the effort.

- 2kg quinces, washed and cut into eighths
- Juice of 6 lemons
- Approximately 1.8kg sugar

Method

Cover the quinces in water and simmer until soft. Drain the liquid and leave the fruit to cool.

Now for the hard bit: Rub the fruit through a sieve to form a puree. Weigh the amount of puree you've made and return it to the cleaned saucepan, adding 450g sugar for every 600g of puree. Stir over a low heat to dissolve the sugar and then turn to a medium heat to cook the puree until it turns a glorious deep orange. Keep stirring so that it doesn't catch and be careful, as it will bubble and spit. When the mixture pulls away so that you can see the bottom of the saucepan, test to see if it has reached the setting point. (As with the medlar jelly (page 240), place a blob on a fridge-cooled saucer for two minutes, though at this point you want it to set firmly, not just wrinkle.) I like to make a hard sliceable 'cheese', so I cook it for a further 15 minutes until it becomes very dark and thick.

Pour into a shallow tin lined with parchment paper and keep in the fridge for up to a month.

Bulb planting part 1 – Garlic

Despite the grim weather (it's chilly and has been drizzling all morning), I have a spare 20 minutes, so I will force myself to go outside and plant some garlic. You can plant garlic any time between late autumn and early winter, but it benefits from having a cold snap to give it a kick-start before spring arrives. That said, you don't want to leave it too late as it's impossible to push the cloves into the ground when it's frozen solid. It's a balancing act. If I had a bit more time, I would get my tulip bulbs in too, but I'll have to do that another day – hopefully when it's a bit brighter.

I wouldn't be without garlic, even though it's widely available, because I find that most shop-bought varieties lack flavour. It's amazing to think it's one of the world's oldest crops, and was worshipped by the Egyptians as a god, as well as being used as local currency. (This might explain why six bulbs were discovered in the tomb of Egyptian pharaoh Tutankhamun, who ruled from 1332 BC to 1323 BC.) I grow it for the younger bulbs, or 'wet garlic' (also known as green garlic, spring onions or garlic scallions), which taste delicious and are a welcome early-spring bounty that's ready to harvest from March to May. You can buy wet garlic in food shops, but I'd wager it's not widely available outside London, and given that it's whipped out before the new season's planting gets going in earnest and also given the tiny amount of space it takes up, it's a no-brainer. Often unused as the discarded immature bulbs are pulled out of the garlic rows to provide more space for bulbs to plump up, in recent years chefs and home cooks, in search of more interesting crops, have rediscovered this early seasonal treat.

As the bulbs are young their papery skin hasn't developed, so they don't need to be peeled. Eaten raw, chopped finely and used as you would spring onions, their flavour is subtle and mild (almost nutty) – a real treat. You can roast them too, and as the green stalks are edible, leave those on and simply cut in half or, if not, just cook a little longer. It's the ultimate zero-waste crop and it's worth planting more than you think you might use, because once you try it you'll be hooked. (Bulbs for planting are widely available in garden centres and online nurseries.)

I'm planting my garlic cloves straight into the beds because the soil

is free-draining, but if you have heavy clay it's better to start them off in pots so they're not sitting in the wet over winter. It's a useful crop to fill gaps in the garden because it doesn't need much room, though avoid planting next to asparagus, peas, beans, sage, parsley and strawberries as it will stunt their growth.

Choose a sunny spot and, if needs be, add compost or well-rotted organic matter to the planting area. Garlic is quick and easy to plant because you need to gently push individual cloves just under the soil and around 15cm apart. This can prove too much of a temptation for birds, so cover with horticultural fleece (which can be bought at garden centres or hardware stores) or mesh. If it's too wet, start off in 5cm pots indoors. Keep an eye on weeds, which can be an issue. Add sulphate of potash in February as a nutrient boost – if you or your friends have wood fires, you can use the ash from them, but do not use coal ash.

If you're leaving some bulbs to mature into standard garlic, make sure to water them if it's been a hot, dry spring and early summer, and then don't water from June onwards. Aim to harvest when the leaves start to fade, which should be towards the end of July. Gently pull up and let them 'set' on the soil surface, though if it's wet, lay on wire mesh or a slatted greenhouse shelf. Watch out for rust, or small brown/orange spots – it's not too much of an issue, and you can spray with sulphur compounds to help protect the garlic cloves inside.

The two types of common garlic are softneck and hardneck, which refers to a biological difference: In softnecks, the stalks are actually a collection of leaves whereas in hardneck varieties, it's a central stem that hardens when the bulbs reach maturity. However, it's probably more useful to understand that softnecks mature more quickly, have a larger number of cloves (up to 18), store well and, as they won't cope in colder temperatures unless protected, are better suited to warmer southern regions. Try 'Solent Wight', 'Early Purple Wight' and 'Picardy Wight'.

Hardnecks, on the other hand, offer two crops for the price of one as they produce scapes – or a tender stem with flower bud, which appears before the bulb has reached maturity. Snip them off and eat raw or sautéed, either way it's a win-win because you're helping the plant by allowing its energy to be directed back into the bulb, rather than a flower, enabling it to produce anything up to 10 cloves, which tend to be bigger than softneck cloves. Try 'Chesnok White' and 'Carcassonne Wight'.

Walking on the wild side

When it comes to foraging for wild garlic, my rule of thumb is to wade – carefully – as far into the carpet of the young, tender leaves as you can. Keep away from path edges and tree trunks, where the young leaves, which is what you want to pick, are less likely to be soaked in dog pee. Just saying.

Kale for pasta, and **leeks** and **bay** in a risotto.

Bulb planting part 2 – Tulips

Autumn comes with plenty of bulb-planting advice. Getting them in the ground while you still can (in other words, when the ground hasn't frozen rock-solid yet) is obviously significant, but in terms of tulips, November turns out to be the sweet spot – landing in-between October, which is generally regarded as the best month for planting as the soil still has some warmth, and December, when you might not be able to dig a hole. Bulbs actually need to go through a dormant period and cold temperatures, which makes sense, given that tulips originally grew in the Himalayas.

November is said to be late enough to avoid a disease called tulip fire, which is a fungal disease that produces brown spots and distorts the leaves so they look as if they've been scorched by fire, hence the name. It's thought that planting now, when the soil is cold but not frozen, reduces the risk.

It's easy to overlook the benefits of planting bulbs. Unlike plugs or more mature plants, it can feel unsatisfactory, as you won't see the results for a month or two. But trust me, as someone who has skipped a year here and there and then lived to regret it, there is nothing like watching the fresh green shoots tentatively emerge through the soil in the depths of winter when there is little other sign of life, not to mention the sheer glory of the spring flowers themselves. At the start of the growing season, any and all signs of activity bring such a feeling of hope and anticipation it's as good for the mind and soul as it is your plot. While tulips might not be edible (I have read that some types are, but I don't feel the need

to explore this), for me, the burst of colour is reason enough to include these beauties in my veg plot.

There is a snag with tulips, though, because they don't all come back the following year, so it can be an annual investment. Having said that, there are some varieties and species that are better than others in making a repeat performance, so it's worth looking out for them. But it really comes down to the rich reward of having colour and interest that only a spring garden can bring. So if you can set aside a little budget for bulbs, it's really worth it.

I'm adding tulips and alliums into the borders and a few pots, but in other years, I have put more thought into displays and combinations of bulbs for containers and window boxes too. It requires a bit of planning and effort, but it really pays off once they start to flower. You can find early spring bloomers, which appear in late January and February, providing a welcome food source for early emerging bees – one year I created more than seven different pots for a magazine feature with this brief. If you're planting in the soil, it's a good idea to lay them out, or, for a more naturalised look, throw them gently on top of the soil and plant them where they fall.

This year I've added 30 more tulips (10 'White Prince' and 20 'Laptop', which is a deep mauve) and 10 ornamental alliums (5 'Violet Beauty' and 5 'Purple Sensation') and I'm excited to see how they'll look dotted in-between the crops. I also came across a few other bulbs that were starting to sprout, so I should see a good splash of colour. I planted several terracotta pots with single colours and added a handful of bulbs into the large myrtle tree container. Take the time to peruse specialist catalogues and websites because, as Anna Pavord declares in her acclaimed book, *The Tulip*, more than a million bulbs might be sold every day, but these are largely dominated by 20 cultivars, and if you're buying a tulip as a cut flower, the chances are you'll be choosing from one of ten cultivars. This seems an opportunity wasted, so I would recommend searching beyond what's available in your local DIY store or garden centre chain. I also thoroughly recommend reading *The Tulip*, which took Pavord seven years to research and is a truly fascinating insight into the history and remarkable story of this humble bulb, complete with beautiful illustrations.

It's worth noting that if yours is a garden often visited by squirrels, it might be best to avoid tulips and crocuses (or protect them), as they are very partial to these varieties, and instead look at narcissus and hyacinths, which are unappetising.

Most bulbs have contractile roots: as they grow, the roots pull them downwards to the appropriate depth. This is really helpful for beginner gardeners, because their adventitious roots will help you out if you haven't planted them deep enough. This is because new bulbs, or corms, develop at a higher level than the 'parent' bulb, so the roots that develop at the base help redress this by shortening, and drawing it deeper into the soil, where the temperature is likely to be more stable, thus providing the optimum planting level.

It's a bit of a gamble, but you can plant spring bulbs as late as December, if the weather has stayed mild enough to get them in the ground. The upside is, bulbs are usually on offer in December, so you can get more for your money!

Kale, **leeks** and **bay**. Kale and leeks are welcome home-grown greens, although it was just a few kale leaves and one leek, which I mixed with goat's cheese as a topping for baked potatoes. I made a lovely pear and bay cake, by the incredibly talented cook Claire Thomson. It's a super recipe that kids love, although it's a more sophisticated flavour combination.

Planting wildlings

I had a gorgeous walk with Teddy this morning. Beautiful blue skies and the first hard frost (not quite a hoar frost), so the grass crunched satisfyingly underfoot. I arrived home to find my pea seedlings ('Dulce Provence') had been delivered too. Bliss. (Though I'm not quite sure what the delivery guy had against them, but I imagine he didn't like eating peas as a kid because the box was ripped and the seedlings were tangled up in a pile at the bottom. Luckily, only two were snapped and the rest were salvageable.) Dog washed (the deepest muddy puddles hadn't quite frozen), kettle on and bread in the toaster, I hot-footed it out to the greenhouse to plant the seedlings. It's such a great feeling to be able to get something started ahead of spring. Had I wanted to have sweet peas in the garden next year, it would be worth getting them going now too.

Job done, but still feeling 'in the zone', I was distracted by random groups of rogue seedlings that have sprung up all over the garden. Self-sown (or uninvited, depending on how you look at it) purple top verbena, calendula 'Indian Prince', mint and strawberries are boldly staking their claim to patches of earth, jostling for position in next summer's display. Although I usually consign them to the compost bin, carelessly thrown away alongside weeds and spent flowers, today I potted up this free garden bounty – they might be useful to plug gaps or pass on to friends and family.

Coincidently, this afternoon I was commissioned to write a magazine feature: 'What to do to get started a bit early, before the weather warms up in March'. Peas, beans and sweet peas can be sown in February – they're the ultimate eager beavers, bookending winter by a willingness to send up shoots whatever the weather – and self-sown seedlings can also be potted up in that month too (though chances are, marigolds are unlikely to survive the winter), so I had plenty of inspiration to draw on.

Kale, leeks and **bay**. I made kale crisps – by sprinkling roughly shredded leaves with oil and salt and baking them in the oven. Leeks in a quiche and bay to flavour oven-baked basmati rice.

STRAWBERRY 101

WHILE POTTING UP stray seedlings is a great way to boost your
fruit stock, it's also a good idea
to pot up a few and bring them
undercover for the winter. I
have some wild strawberries in a
hanging basket, and thanks to the
shelter of my greenhouse (a cool
windowsill will work just as well),
they'll produce a bountiful harvest
as much as six weeks earlier than
outdoor-grown berries. If you

grow strawberries in beds outside you won't even need to buy plants
from a garden centre – just dig up a few baby plants that are attached to
the parent on 'runners' and plant them instead.

1. Fill a hanging basket or 20cm-diameter container with multipurpose
   compost. Make three holes in the compost around the edge and
   plant one strawberry plant in each one. Water well and leave in a
   cool greenhouse.

2. Remove leggy runners as they grow – you're trying to encourage the
   plant to put all its energy into producing juicy red fruit rather than
   new young plants.

3. Feed the plants with a seaweed-based fertiliser every fortnight once
   the fruits start to appear.

Keep an eye out for slugs – they'll even appear inside greenhouses and
conservatories. And watch out for the weather: If it's a very hot spring,
you can protect the plants and fruit from scorching under the glass with
a layer of horticultural fleece. That said, strawberries are easy and fun to
grow and a good fruit for kids to try, as they will love the juicy red fruits
as a reward.

Planting wildings

Greenery – edible and ornamental

It's a funny time of year if you're growing crops. It's a bit like the evening before an exam: There's nothing more you can do – you either know it or you don't. There are a few jobs suited to this wintry month, and, if you have access to somewhere warm, you can still sow a few crops, but there's no denying that this is when it's time to down tools. For some, being cooped up indoors is a challenge, but there's plenty to enjoy, even if plants are dormant and there isn't much activity in the garden. It's a good time to reflect on the year's growing season, so the year's successes can be repeated and any mistakes noted and avoided.

While veg beds and containers will feature some seasonal treats from the brassica family, as well as winter salad and some hardy herbs, there are a few wildlife-friendly plants that might be worth trying to squeeze in – you'll be doing a good turn to those small creatures battling the cold, wet weather, as well as adding some colour and texture to your plot at a time when it can feel bare and unloved. Hawthorn and dog roses provide berries, which can be shared with wildlife as well as being used to flavour drinks and syrups, but of course you can also choose varieties like sunflowers and teasels, which flower in late summer and autumn, so that their dying blooms provide a welcome seed snack.

This year, I decided to make an outdoor wreath to add a festive flourish to the garden. I used ivy, myrtle and bay as a glossy green base and added wispy twigs topped with catkins and pussy willow, as well as hydrangeas from a neighbour's garden. As I mentioned, we have two cats, so I wouldn't dream of encouraging birds to take their chances,

but if you don't own cats, why not embellish your wreath with edible treats, like apples, seed heads, berries and even fat balls (there's an easy recipe on page 237). I do make the concession of providing some water on frosty days (the cats don't spend much time outside, so I'm fairly confident thirsty birds and other visiting wildlife will be left in peace to enjoy a drink). Thinking about wildlife also provides the perfect excuse to put tidying up the garden on hold because the chances are you could be disturbing insects, mammals and small creatures that hibernate just under the soil or in piles of dead leaves and twigs.

Chilean guava berries, which we added to a recipe for madeleine cakes; **celery** and **cavolo nero** in a minestrone soup.

Rhubarb

As a child I remember taking a paper bag half-filled with sugar down to the bottom of our garden, where we had several large rhubarb plants. I can still hear the snap as I broke a juicy stem off the plant, before stuffing it into the bag. I don't have a mouth-full of fillings, which is surprising, because I was allowed to do this for as long as the rhubarb lasted. For better or worse, I wouldn't encourage Hal to do this nowadays, so to let him enjoy the delectably fruity-sour treat, I thought I would try forcing rhubarb instead. The idea is to encourage an earlier crop, which is also a bit softer and sweeter than the usual woody stems. As Hal's birthday is in March, I'm aiming to harvest the stems in time to make his favourite pudding, as well as a deliciously zingy cordial.

Rhubarb is a great crop for beginner gardeners because it's perfectly able to cope with the wet, cold weather that we often endure in the UK, and especially in Yorkshire – the region's climate, together with its nutrient-rich soil, was the reason it used to produce 90 per cent of the world's winter rhubarb during the nineteenth century. Yorkshire's forced rhubarb is akin to champagne, in that The Triangle (between Wakefield, Morley and Rothwell) is recognised as a 'Protected Designation of Origin', allowing only a crop from this region to advertise itself as Yorkshire Rhubarb.

Forcing rhubarb transforms it from a tart treat that needs sugar, into a sweeter, softer one that can be eaten raw, as well as cooked. Essentially, the combination of exposing the rhubarb crown to frost breaks its dormancy and spurs the plant to grow and at the same time convert the stored starch (in the crown) into glucose. Usually used by the entire plant, when it's made to grow quickly and in darkness, the glucose remains in the stem and makes it taste sweeter.

How to force

Try 'Early Timperley', which you can get going in late January or early February. If you prefer a little acidity when it comes to the flavour, go for 'Victoria', and if this all sounds like too much hard work, and an early crop isn't that important to you, 'Champagne' produces sweet stems whether forced or not.

Make sure the plants have plenty of nutrients to boost their growth, so dig in lots of well-rotted manure or compost around your rhubarb plant. I don't have a rhubarb, so have bought a corm and am planting it

Rhubarb, rhubarb, rhubarb

In the true spirit of horticulturists the world over, John Oldroyd, head of one of the oldest families involved in forcing rhubarb, was taught this dark art in the 1920s by a friend and local rhubarb grower in exchange for sharing his knowledge about growing strawberries. In what sounds like the start of a children's book, in the vast barns located in a nine-acre patch of land that falls between Wakefield, Morley and Rothwell, farmers tiptoe about, picking rhubarb by candlelight, to ensure the delicate pink stems aren't exposed to light and end up photosynthesising. It's an incredible sight, and if you're ever in the area, it's well worth making a trip to see for yourself or to enjoy the Wakefield Food, Drink and Rhubarb Festival, which takes place towards the end of February. While it sounds like one of those delightfully quirky British traditions, there is a grittier side to the story. It is agriculture after all, and as such, back-breaking work: cuttings are taken from mature plants, grown on for two years and then brought indoors to be forced and ultimately picked by hand, all of which is extremely labour intensive.

in a large bucket. I'll need another bucket to cover the plant in order to block out the light. If you use a large pot, be sure to cover the drainage hole so that it prevents light from getting inside. Insulate the top bucket with bubble wrap, carpet or straw (pile it up all over the 'lid') as this warms the air inside and encourages the plant to put on some growth. Don't be tempted to fill the bucket with straw, as it can encourage botrytis and make the stems taste of mould, as straw can be a shelter for fungal spores.

I'm starting my plant off a bit early because I'm hoping a month or two extra might just help compensate for the fact it isn't already established in the ground. In theory, you can divide rhubarb at this time of year, so it might be OK. Traditionally, however, you would be starting to force your rhubarb later in the season, perhaps the end of January, early February. If all goes to plan, you should be able to harvest after eight weeks, when the stems are about 20–30cm long. Pull stems gently from the base and be aware that the leaves are poisonous, so remove them before cooking.

This is a fairly intensive process for the plant, so let them grow on in peace, without forcing them again, for the rest of the year and the following. If you're a rhubarb-a-holic – and you have the space – perhaps it's worth having two or more plants on the go. Plants will look a bit unruly after a couple of years – not to worry, simply dig them up in the autumn and divide the roots (or corms) into two or three chunks. Either replant for more rhubarb or give away to friends.

Rhubarb tips

- Do not harvest rhubarb in the heat, as the stalks will quickly wilt.
- It's better to pull rather than cut stalks when you harvest them, as cutting encourages rot.
- Always leave a few stalks on the plant to ensure it remains productive.

Rhubarb

Tools

For years, setting aside a few hours to clean the garden tools and tidy the greenhouse would appear at the bottom of my to-do list, if at all. With only a limited amount of time to spend in the garden around work and family life, I couldn't help feeling it would be better to do more productive jobs, like planting or sowing. Eventually the frustration at not being able to lay my hands on my gardening knife without first having to rummage through several boxes, or finding that my secateurs were getting harder to use as the rust patches worsened, made me rethink my approach. These days, as the year draws to a close and there's less to do in the garden, an annual winter clean has become a satisfying ritual that feels just as rewarding as gently prodding seeds into a tray of compost. I find it a mindful practice, too. I'm listening to Christmas carols as I clean down my collection of hand tools, spades and forks in hot soapy water, dry them off and then hang them back on their hooks or prop them in their allocated places against the wall. It's nice to remember when and how I last used them and the jobs I'll need them for once the weather warms. I don't oil everything, but if the metal looks like it could do with a bit of TLC, I use a cloth to rub in some olive oil. Fine sandpaper keeps my secateur blades in good working order, followed by an application of oil, which ensures they cut smoothly.

There is method behind the apparent madness of cleaning tools – strictly speaking, dirt and soil should be removed after each use. While in practice that's not realistic, keeping on top of it is a good idea. It's important to look after your kit, as dirty blades can infect or cross-contaminate plants with insect eggs or weed seeds. Pots and seed trays need a thorough clean too, because dried soil and dirt can harbour

disease and cause problems for new plants the following season. Use a dry, stiff brush to remove as much as you can and then wash them in warm soapy water. Leave to dry and then stack them ready for use next year.

If you have an area where you keep your gardening paraphernalia, either a shelf, cupboard, greenhouse or shed, then I would urge you to give it a good clean too. It's an opportunity to reacquaint yourself with all the bits and bobs you have accumulated over the year: organise seeds into the months they can be sown, discard the out-of-date packets and untangle balls of string so that you're ready to find exactly what you need the moment the weather warms come the spring. If you have a bigger space, like a greenhouse, it's sensible to choose a dry day so that you can pull everything outside to give it a thorough clean.

Useful tools

SOIL SIEVE Gorgeous to look at when they're hanging up in the shed, this is a really practical bit of kit that helps create a fine soil to cover seeds in pots and trays if you're not using vermiculite. You can buy new ones, but you can't beat the worn, wooden vintage styles. If you're doing a larger job and need to sieve whole wheelbarrows of soil, why not make your own? Make two rectangular timber frames, a little larger than the barrow, sandwich mesh in-between them and fix in place with screws.

TRUG A trug is a great addition to a potting shed as you can use it for so many different jobs; carry your tools out into the garden, fill it with green waste when you're tidying the garden or soak bare-rooted plants in it, prior to planting out.

POTTING BENCH TRAY If you don't have the luxury of a potting bench, this tray is a useful alternative that can be placed on any flat surface. It's the only way to tackle a seed-sowing session and keep all your compost in one area. They're available in plastic, metal or wooden designs, so you can choose one to suit your pocket.

GARDEN KNIFE A small fold-away knife is a lifesaver in the garden. Whether you're taking cuttings, nicking a rogue sucker off a raspberry cane or opening a bag of compost, it's all you'll need. Again, they come in a range of styles, with plastic, metal or wooden handles, but it's a good idea to try it out and hold it in your hand before you buy it, to make sure it feels comfortable. If you don't like the idea of maintaining your tools, go for a stainless steel rather than carbon steel blade, as it won't rust.

HOE For a speedy way to keep on top of weeds in your garden, find a hoe that works for you. They come in a range of designs – from a Dutch hoe with a forward-facing blade that cuts through established and seedling weeds to a half-moon hoe that helps access awkward parts of a border. Smaller hand hoes are also useful for more focused work.

Dried **myrtle** to become a swanky alternative to black peppercorns; **celery** in a veggie Bolognese sauce; **savoy cabbage** simply shredded and sautéed in butter and garlic.

Apples and myrtle

I usually store my apple harvest individually wrapped in newspaper and laid out in layers in a cardboard box somewhere cool for up to five months (although ours have always been eaten before then). This year I've borrowed my friend's dehydrator so I can transform the last of our apples into delicious chewy, dried apple rings. I'm also going to try drying the crop of myrtle berries, which really need to be picked because they are weighing down the delicate branches of the tree, and use them as a substitute for peppercorns. I'm hoping that there will be enough to give as Christmas presents, too.

It's satisfying to finally harvest the berries. I was beginning to feel sad when I looked out from the kitchen and saw the myrtle tree's drooping branches, like an old lady who, though stooped, stoically continues her daily routine. However, it's so cold today, I can only stay outside for 10 minutes at a time before I have to pop back into the warmth of the house to defrost my hands. Hal joined me for a bit, but it's a fiddly job with tiny frozen fingers. We end up filling three ice-cream containers and there are still plenty of berries left on the tree for the female blackbird who visits every afternoon. Back in the kitchen, I remove rogue leaves, mini spiders and stalks and tip them into the dehydrator trays – I haven't used one before, but I spread them out, one berry deep, to allow air to circulate. Looking at the heat and temperature guide in the handbook, I'm guessing they'll need the same treatment as strawberries and cherries (the smallest fruits they include – they don't mention myrtle berries, funnily enough). I opt for six hours at 70°C. Yesterday I tried a small batch in my oven, set at 100°C, but left them in too long and ended up with charred rather than dried berries. If you can set your oven between

50°C and 100°C, you won't have to buy a dehydrator to enjoy the fun of drying fruit, vegetables and herbs, but do keep a close watch on them, checking each hour to see how much more drying they need.

I core and slice the last of the apples so that they're about 5mm thick, and brush them with lemon juice to prevent them from discolouring during the drying process. I lay them out on the trays in the same way, with plenty of space for the air to circulate. I've also put them on the same temperature setting as the berries, for six hours – Hal and I prefer them to be chewy rather than crunchy.

A note about storage

Unless you're lucky enough to have an allotment or oodles of space, I don't think you'll need to rely on too many storage techniques to ensure your harvests last the winter. While traditional-style clamps (a pit covered with sand used for storing carrots, turnips and other root vegetables) are fun to make, think of it as one less job to do, and in terms of zero waste, there's nothing like freshly picking and eating your crops in season. If you do find yourself with a glut of something and you're not pickling, freezing or drying them, the key thing to remember is to wrap them individually and check them regularly – one rotten item can spoil the remainder of the harvest. In theory, they should last four to five months, but this will depend on the particular storage conditions you have.

Growing apples

Now's the time to plant bare-root fruit trees, or in other words, trees that are grown in the ground rather than containers, and are dug up when they are dormant (from November to March), to be dispatched to customers during these months only. If you can only find space for one tree, they're a great addition to the garden, providing height (even dwarf varieties will introduce a bit of vertical interest), spring blossom, which attracts bees and other pollinating insects, and dappled shade, which can be welcome if your plot is in full sun.

Bare-root trees tend to be the choice of professional growers because they are better value for money for any given height and size of plant compared to their containerised counterparts, they tend to establish more quickly because a larger surface area of the roots is in direct contact with the soil, and less packaging means they are more environmentally friendly. There's also the added advantage that there's a bigger choice of bare-root varieties to choose from. That's not to say that container-grown trees are bad – in fact, being grown this way means they can be planted all year round, so that's good news if you've missed the winter window.

Another great reason to grow fruit trees is that they can be trained in certain shapes, which allows them to fit into tight spots or provide structural interest in a small space. If you look at pictures of old walled

gardens, you will see fan-trained fruit against the brick walls, where the branches of the trees are quite literally tied against a wooden structure or along wires to encourage them to grow in a fan shape. There are also espalier trees that are trained to grow in horizontal layers, which make a beautiful alternative to traditional shrub hedges and really help maximise limited space. They also provide an attractive structural shape during the winter months, which is lovely if there's not much else in the garden.

I have three espalier apple trees, originally grown in large square containers to form a screen that separated the patio from the rest of the garden. I moved them a couple of years ago, planting them in the ground against one of the side walls, and they've settled in well to their new position. I'd advise buying two-year-old whips (young trees), which have been started off as espaliers, though maiden trees are cheaper and you can always search online or get advice on how to prune and train them from the grower.

Once their shape is established, they require little in the way of pruning, apart from cutting back unwanted side-shoots growing from the main horizontal 'leader' (or stem) in July or August, to help restrict growth and provide plenty of light to let the fruit ripen. When I planted them in both the containers and then the ground, I added in plenty of well-rotted organic matter and hammered a stake into the planting hole to help secure the tree.

Fruit trees are grown on rootstock (the root and stem of a related tree), as this helps control their ultimate size and vigour, which is important if you're considering how much room you have for a tree or two. The apple tree dwarf stocks M27, M9 and M26 (the M referring to the East Malling Research Station where the rootstocks were developed in the 1920s) are becoming increasingly popular, with patio fruit trees the perfect solution for tiny gardens, and it is M26 that is generally used for espaliers. The rootstock known as MM106 is a semi-dwarf stock, which has been used in orchards to help match the machinery and make the process of picking more efficient. Then there are MM111 and M25, which are vigorous and mature into large specimens. When planting, make sure the 'graft point', or the bulge where the rootstock and your chosen tree were fused together, is kept above the soil level, and then regularly water throughout the year. Under-watering is a common mistake, and even when it's rained, a watering can of water won't go amiss – trees are a considerable outlay, so a bit of extra effort will ensure it thrives and matures. In terms of care, an annual feed of a balanced fertiliser is important, as well as some sulphate of potash to encourage plenty of flowers and ultimately fruit. Mulch in spring to help lock in moisture and suppress weeds that compete for water and nutrients. You can also hang pheromone traps in apple and plum trees to reduce codling moth.

The old ones are the best...

...as I'm now inclined to think, being the wrong side of 45! On a more serious note, I do think it's often the case that old, or heritage, fruit and vegetable varieties are better. There is, of course, a lot to commend disease-resistant hybrid mash-ups, but the innovation is often at the expense of taste. Old-fashioned varieties, grown before the advent of commercial growing in the 1920s, also suit the home grower better than those created for a commercial market – for example, freshly picked tomatoes don't need to have the tougher, thicker skin required by the varieties that are transported from country to country. It stands to reason that there is a different set of priorities to satisfy the rigorous commercial market, whereas for the home grower, taste is ultimately king. Some heritage fruit and vegetables tell an even more specific story and are linked to a particular region with its unique soil, temperatures and moisture levels. Apples are an example of this, and where you are in the country – Herefordshire, Worcestershire or Kent, for example – will determine which varieties you can grow. Heritage vegetables introduce a fascinating aspect to choosing what you're going to grow, and connect you to the past – perhaps you might find out what your grandparents or great-grandparents grew in their vegetable plots, or rediscover varieties that were traditionally grown in the region in which you grew up. I love the sound of the dessert apple, 'Pig's Nose Pippin', which dates back to 1884 and was grown in my home city of Hereford. Other well-known varieties include 'Worcester Pearmain', 'Ribston Pippin' and 'Cornish Aromatic'.

Growing myrtle

The container-grown myrtle I have in a large pot in my back yard proves there are no hard and fast rules when it comes to gardening. With dense, glossy evergreen leaves, myrtles are more commonly used as shrubs for hedging, as their leaves look neat and clean after pruning, but they can be grown as small trees, too. (In his 1722 book *The City Gardener*, the original city gardener, Thomas Fairchild, notes that myrtle was reintroduced in England in the sixteenth century, with the return from Spain in 1585 of Sir Walter Raleigh, who also brought with him the first orange trees. At the time of writing, Fairchild comments that myrtle was commonly rented from nurserymen on a temporary basis, used to fill empty fireplaces during the warm months each year.) I bought mine as a standard tree, where the branches along the lower section of the stem are removed, leaving those of the top section to be pruned into a lollipop shape. Over the last three years I haven't pruned it at all, allowing the branches to grow as they wish. The result is a gorgeous, elegant specimen, which transports me to the Mediterranean whenever I look at it because it has the same lovely open shape as an olive tree, with a similarly textured bark that looks parched by the sun, and long, languid branches (can branches be languid?) that gently sway in the breeze.

Myrtle produces sweet-smelling flowers during the summer, which pollinators absolutely adore, followed by dark purple edible little berries in late autumn, which in its native Sardinia and Corsica are macerated in alcohol to make the popular aperitif mirto. The aromatic flavour – a little like juniper – is a match made in heaven when it's teamed with buttery savoy cabbage.

While this is a tender variety that won't appreciate cold, wet weather, I've found that it copes perfectly well in my relatively sheltered small city garden. If you're in a part of the country that has sharper temperatures, then it won't do any harm to wrap it in horticultural fleece or something similar during very cold spells. Happy in most soil types, as long as they're well-draining, it will do best in a sunny, sheltered position.

Bay for flavouring soup and a handful of **myrtle** berries to experiment with infusing a small bottle of gin.

Frost

My sister is coming tomorrow to take photographs for our winter shoot – it's a lovely excuse to get out into the garden because it has rained a lot over the last few days and there hasn't been a chance to do much more than pick up the odd dog poop.

This morning a mild frost had covered the kale and cavolo nero with a dusting of sparkling white crystals. The forecast is for it to be more severe tonight, which is great news and hopefully means we can get some glorious wintry shots in the bag.

Generally speaking, frost isn't especially welcome in a garden. It might transform the countryside's rolling hills and endless fields into an enchanting landscape, but the reality for lots of gardeners is that tender cherished plants might suffer damage, or even be lost altogether to Jack Frost's icy touch.

Whether or not your plants suffer is down to their ability to create their own antifreeze (in other words, sugar and amino acids) once the days start to shorten in the autumn. By doing this, they are able to lower the freezing point of their cells, which allows them to withstand the drop in temperature. For those plants unable to perform this preemptive trick, when temperatures fall below 0°C, water naturally held in the plant cells will freeze, which in turn damages the cell wall as it expands and then contracts – you can see the signs if plants are limp and blackened. (Technically, temperatures between 0°C and -2°C will produce a light frost, which affects some crops like beans, tomatoes, peppers and pumpkins, whereas root vegetables and onions should be able to cope. When temperatures fall below -2°C, however, it becomes a hard frost, which is more damaging.)

Luckily, I don't have either tender crops or dainty herbaceous plants to worry about, but if I had, it would be worth getting into the routine of checking the weather forecast for signs of frost and then wrapping any vulnerable specimens in either a layer or two of horticultural fleece, or sheets of newspaper, which you then stuff with crumpled newspaper or straw, being careful not to damage the plant. It's a good idea to make covers that you can lift on and off easily, so that the plant can warm up as the following day's temperatures rise. I have read that farmers spray crops with water prior to a frost because it turns into ice and thus provides a protective layer against colder air temperatures – I haven't tried this myself and imagine the process is more involved than just turning on your hose. Container-grown plants can be moved to somewhere sheltered or under cover if you have a shed, garage or greenhouse, while celery, spinach and chard would appreciate being covered in straw to offer some protection.

I do, however, have a garden with several crop varieties that actually benefit from a short, sharp blast of sub-zero temperatures: my leafy and stem crops like leeks, Brussels sprouts and kale, taste sweeter after frosts, as do roots like beets, carrots, turnips and parsnips. These crops produce the antifreeze mentioned above, which, in their case, produces sugars.

Don't be caught out by late spring and early autumn frosts. The former can ruin a crop by damaging spring blossoms and young fruits and the latter can wipe out the last of your crops. Keep an eye on the weather forecasts and have a layer of protection at the ready.

Happy Christmas! And this year it was much happier, as we harvested our one **broccoli** stem and a bit of **kale** to accompany that Christmas classic: veggie cannelloni. A fitting end to a year of humble harvests from our small city plot.

Acknowledgements

Julie – I'll be forever grateful that you considered my proposal in the first place, and then that you were happy to spend time working out how we could make it the book we've produced today. Liz, thank you for transforming my ramblings into complete, grammatically correct sentences; and Jenny, it's been such a pleasure to work with you and your brilliant team at Bloomsbury, who have fine-tuned *City Veg* and made it such a beautiful book.

To my family and friends: Hal and I are lucky to have you in our lives – you know who you are and we wouldn't be here, happily growing veg, without you all. That said, Mum and Dad, thank you for being such a wonderful 'pillowcase'; WAA & UP, without you, we wouldn't have the garden to grow everything in – thank you won't ever quite cover it, but thank you; The Collinseses – once again you've coped brilliantly with Tory popping up to Bristol at the drop of a hat … though I think next time, you need to send up your delicious suppers and cookies, please. And Tory – you're the best big sister a girl could wish for, and a pretty darn talented photographer, too. I'm so proud of the second book we've made together.

Recommended reading and viewing

The Biggest Little Farm, John Chester, dir. (Neon, 2018) [film]

Crawford, M. (2012), *How to Grow Perennial Vegetables*, Cambridge: Green Books

Fairchild, T. (1722), *The City Gardener*, London: T. Woodward

Mann, C. (2011), *1493: Uncovering the New World Columbus Created*, London: Granta

McTernan, C. (2015), *One-Pot Gourmet Gardener*, London: Frances Lincoln

Middleton, C.H. and Heath, A. (1942), *From Garden to Kitchen*, London: Cassell

Mollison, B. (1988), *Permaculture: A Designer's Manual*, Sisters Creek, Australia: Tagari

Pavord, A. (1999), *The Tulip*, London: Bloomsbury

Rebanks, J. (2020), *English Pastoral*, London: Penguin

Rebanks, J. (2016), *The Shepherd's Life*, London: Penguin

Thompson, K. (2011), *An Ear To The Ground*, London: Penguin

Wulf, A. (2015), *The Invention of Nature*, London: John Murray

Resources

gourmetmushrooms.co.uk – supplier of mushroom kits
mushroombox.co.uk – supplier of mushroom kits
rhs.org.uk – the go-to site for horticultural advice and information
rusticmushrooms.co.uk – supplier of mushroom kits
wigglywigglers.com – supplier of worms and wormeries
zwia.org – Zero Waste International Alliance

Cultivated plant varieties mentioned in this book

'Alabaster' (celeriac)
'Ariane' (asparagus)
'Autumn Bliss' (raspberry)
'Autumn Gold' (onion)
'Backlim' (asparagus)

'Banana Legs' (tomato)
'Beauregard' (sweet potato)
'Ben Lomond' (blackcurrant)
'Ben Sarek' (blackcurrant)

'Big Brandy' (tomato)
'Black Cherry' (tomato)
'Black Magic' (cavolo nero)
'Blenheim Orange' (melon)

'Blue Fortune' (Mexican giant hyssop)
'Bright lights' (chard)
'Brilliant' (celeriac)
'Capucijner' (pea)
'Carcassonne Wight' (garlic)
'Carolina Ruby' (sweet potato)
'Champagne' (rhubarb)
'Charity' (pelargonium/ geranium)
'Chartreuse de Parme' (hybrid tea rose)
'Chesnok White' (garlic)
'Cornichon de Paris' (cucumber)
'Costoluto Fiorentino' (tomato)
'Crown Prince' (squash)
'De Monica' (broad bean)
'Dieta' (broad bean)
'Double Red' (sweetcorn)
'Douce Provence' (pea)
'Dwarf Sunray' (Jerusalem artichoke)
'Early Purple Wight' (garlic)
'Early Timperley' (rhubarb)
'Figaro' (shallot)
'Fuseau' (Jerusalem artichoke)
'Gardener's Delight' (tomato)
'Giant Prague' (celeriac)
'Gijnlim' (asparagus)
'Giulietta' (tomato)

'Glass Gem' (sweetcorn)
'Glen Ample' (raspberry)
'Glen Prosen' (raspberry)
'Golden Everest' (raspberry)
'Green Globe' (globe artichoke)
'Hero of Lockinge' (melon)
'Invicta' (gooseberry)
'Ishikura' (onion)
'Jermor' (shallot)
'Junifer' (redcurrant)
'Lady Scarborough' (pelargonium/ geranium)
'Laptop' (tulip)
'Lemon Tree' (tomato)
'Leveller' (gooseberry)
'Mabel Grey' (pelargonium/ geranium)
'Mars' (celeriac)
'Meteor' (pea)
'Monarch' (celeriac)
'Moneymaker' (tomato)
'Munchkin' (pumpkin)
'Picardy Wight' (garlic)
'Prinz' (celeriac)
'Purple Sensation' (allium)
'Rat's Tail' (radish)
'Red Baron' (onion)
'Red Pear' (tomato)
'Rocket' (potato)
'Rovada' (redcurrant)
'Ruby Beauty' (raspberry)
'Senshyu' (onion)
'Shakespeare' (onion)
'Sibley's Patio Medlar'

(medlar)
'Sibley's Patio Quince' (quince)
'Snobaby' F1 (sweetcorn)
'Solent Wight' (garlic)
'Special Swiss' (sweetcorn)
'Starlight' (raspberry)
'Stewart's Purple' (asparagus)
'Sturon' (onion)
'Sungold' (tomato)
'Swift' (potato)
'Tigerella' (tomato)
'Torrento' (pelargonium/ geranium)
'Versailles Blanche' (whitecurrant)
'Victoria' (rhubarb)
'Violet Beauty' (allium)
'Violetta di Chioggia' (globe artichoke)
'Waverex' (pea)
'White Lisbon' (onion)
'White Prince' (tulip)
'Yummy' (raspberry)
'Zebrina' (mallow)

Scientific names of plants and insects mentioned in this book

I have used scientific names here and there, not to try and sound unnecessarily scholarly, but rather to clarify the exact type of plant I'm growing or writing about – common names are all well and good, but they can (and do) lead to confusion (marigolds are a case in point: *Calendula officinalis* is the type of marigold you want to grow in an edible garden, whereas other types of marigold aren't necessarily edible; swedes and turnips also illustrate the point, because to the Scots, a turnip can also be called a swede!). Thankfully Carl Linneaus came up with a new system of naming organisms in the mid 1700s, known as binominal nomenclature, which gave a species a name composed of two parts and essentially put a stop to potential misunderstandings about any given species. In doing so, he earned himself the rather fitting – if not unimaginative – nickname, 'the father of modern taxonomy'.

Acmella oleracea: electric daisy

Allium hollandicum (aflatunense): ornamental allium

Allium stipitatum: allium 'White Giant'

Althaea rosea: hollyhock

Amelanchier lamarckii: amelanchier

Anemone × hybrida: Japanese anemones or Honorine Jobert

Aphidoletes aphidimyza: small midge or aphid midge

Arbutus unedo: strawberry tree, cane apple, Dalmatian strawberry or Killarney strawberry

Arion ater: black slug

Begonia x tuberhybrida: tuberous begonia

Brassica oleracea longata: giant Jersey kale or walking-stick cabbage

Convolvulaceae: morning glory family or bindweed

Dioscorea: yam

Hemerocallis: daylily

Laurus nobilis: bay tree

Limax maximus: leopard slug or great grey slug

Malus x domestica: apple tree

Myrtus communis: myrtle tree

Pelargonium graveolens: rose-scented geranium

Pelargonium quercifolia: pine-scented geranium

Pelargonium tomentosum: peppermint-scented geranium

Pelargoniums fragrans: sweet-scented geranium

Sambucus nigra: elderflower or elder 'Eva'

Solanum tuberosum: common potato

Sorghum nigrum: black millet

Tanacetum cinerariifolium: pyrethrum daisy, insect powder plant or Dalmatia pyrethrum

Verbena bonariensis: tall verbena, purple top, Argentinian vervain or South American vervain

Index